AUTIPOWER!

Successful Living and Working with
an Autism Spectrum Disorder

of related interest

Autism All-Stars
How We Use Our Autism and Asperger Traits to Shine in Life
Edited by Josie Santomauro
Foreword by Tony Attwood
ISBN 978 1 84310 188 8
eISBN 978 0 85700 600 4

The Complete Guide to Getting a Job for People with Asperger's Syndrome
Find the Right Career and Get Hired
Barbara Bissonnette
ISBN 978 1 84905 921 3
eISBN 978 0 85700 692 9

Asperger's Syndrome Workplace Survival Guide
A Neurotypical's Secrets for Success
Barbara Bissonnette
Foreword by Yvona Fast
ISBN 978 1 84905 943 5
eISBN 978 0 85700 807 7

How to Find Work that Works for People with Asperger Syndrome
The Ultimate Guide for Getting People with Asperger Syndrome into the Workplace (and keeping them there!)
Gail Hawkins
ISBN 978 1 84310 151 2

Aspies on Mental Health
Speaking for Ourselves
Edited by Luke Beardon and Dean Worton
ISBN 978 1 84905 152 1
eISBN 978 0 85700 287 7
Part of the Adults Speak Out about Asperger Syndrome series

Asperger Syndrome and Anxiety
A Guide to Successful Stress Management
Nick Dubin
Foreword by Valerie Gaus
ISBN 978 1 84310 895 5
eISBN 978 1 84642 922 4

AUTIPOWER!

Successful Living and Working with an Autism Spectrum Disorder

HERMAN JANSEN AND BETTY ROMBOUT

TRANSLATED BY KARIN LEMMEN

Jessica Kingsley *Publishers*
London and Philadelphia

First published in 2014
by Jessica Kingsley Publishers
73 Collier Street
London N1 9BE, UK
and
400 Market Street, Suite 400
Philadelphia, PA 19106, USA

First published in Dutch in 2011 by Uitgeverij Pepijn, The Netherlands

www.jkp.com

Library of Congress Cataloging in Publication Data
Jansen, Herman, 1963-
  [Autipower. English]
  Autipower! : successful living and working with an autism spectrum disorder /
Herman Jansen and
Betty Rombout ; translated by Karin Lemmen.
    pages cm
  ISBN 978-1-84905-437-9 (alk. paper)
  1. Autistic people--Netherlands--Case studies. 2. Autism spectrum disorders-
-Case studies. I. Rombout,
Betty, 1962- II. Title.
  RC553.A88J356613 2014
  616.85'882--dc23
                          2013042042

British Library Cataloguing in Publication Data
A CIP catalogue record for this book is available from the British Library

ISBN 978 1 84905 437 9
eISBN 978 0 85700 869 5

Printed and bound in Great Britain by Bell & Bain Ltd, Glasgow

CONTENTS

INTRODUCTION

AutiPower! does not contain a step-by-step plan for people with an autism spectrum disorder (ASD) to become successful. We do not think such a step-by-step plan exists. We have talked extensively to people with ASD, and they are all happy in their own way. Opinions on success differ. Some people feel very successful because they make the most of their lives; there are impairments *and* possibilities. For others, there is still room for improvement.

The only role that we gave ourselves as authors was to write down what people told us. That is all. We have not made anything up, we do not analyse and construe, and we do not draw any conclusions. We leave that entirely to the people we interviewed. And apart from people with autism, these included professionals, re-integration experts and employers. Now that the book is finished, the reader, too, can draw his or her own conclusions.

This might give the impression that this book is not instructive. On the contrary, reading the book leads to recognition and new understanding – especially, we hope, of the strengths of people with autism, as we are convinced that these people are exceptionally valuable in our society.

Writing this book was a true journey of exploration for us. As 'neurotypicals', a term we learned from the philosopher with autism, Jan Verhaegh, we engrossed ourselves in a world unknown to us: the world of people with autism. We were captivated from the start. The cordiality with which we were received. The openness. The trust shown to us. Only rarely did we ask a question people preferred not to answer, or which the interviewee did answer, but asked us not to incorporate in the book.

We quickly noticed that people with ASD are special people. They are who they are. 'They can't help themselves,' as Ted de Laat says in the conversation we had with him. That was also the reason why his wife found him attractive when they met. And despite (or maybe even thanks to) his autism, they are still happy together.

Even before the book has reached the shops, we are hearing sceptical comments on the title. *AutiPower!* Isn't that a bit exaggerated? Autism is not all roses. Of course not. Autism is an impairment that should not be underestimated. It is much more than being slightly 'different'. Therefore we do not ignore the problems autism causes for people. These are amply discussed in each interview.

But we are ultimately interested in the 'power' which is revealed in the way people deal with their impairments and in the way they eventually manage to use the qualities autism endows them with. Barbara de Leeuw even calls her ASD (and ADHD) her talent. She says she could never do her work as well if she did not have autism. The 'power' is also visible in the incredible resilience shown by people – Jaap Brand, for example, holding a doctor's degree in mathematics, who had trouble keeping his job but eventually found just what he wanted. We can name a few more examples like these. But you will see them for yourself when you read this book.

Many of the older people with ASD who speak out in this book are glad not to have been branded as 'autistic' when they were young. From an early age, they had to fight for their place in society, unaware of their 'handicap'. That was not an easy road. Lack of understanding, depression, loss of a job; they had much to endure. This book shows that this does not have to happen.

Is it not time we properly valued people with ASD in our society and helped them make the most of themselves? No one should be excluded. We believe in looking at people's abilities rather than their disabilities – by seeing the strengths, the 'power', of people with ASD. *AutiPower!* shows that being successful at work and in life on the autistic spectrum is possible. An autism-friendly society is, however, essential if we are to achieve this. This is not asking too much, especially when one considers how much it will benefit society.

We hope you enjoy reading this book.

1.

THE MAN WHO INVENTED HIMSELF

Jaap Brand (47-years-old) biostatistician and board member of PAS (People on the Autistic Spectrum) an association for gifted people with ASD in the Netherlands (see p.80).

Jaap Brand has a very good memory. For example, he recalls perfectly the events of one day in the past: 15 June 1979. He was 14-years-old at the time. His school was having an open day. The children walked past the different classrooms in small groups, and in each room they were given information about the various subjects they were going to study. They learned how a school day is set up – playfully and informally. Nothing special, really. But for Jaap things turned out differently. He became overexcited and built up so much stress during the day that it erupted at home that evening. He suffered severe crying fits and outbursts of anger. This incident was typical of how his autism manifested itself in the past. In the past? Yes. As the conversation proceeds, it becomes clear that Jaap has developed in a remarkable way. Jaap has invented himself!

He is hardly bothered by bouts of overstimulation any more. *'Overstimulation results from incorrect ways of thinking,'* he explains. *'It's caused by feeling unsafe. You live in a world you don't fully understand. As a result, you regularly clash with this world. In your head, you build an ideal image of how you want to be in the world. For me this meant at that time that I had to be especially tough and funny. I identified myself with James Bond. He always has a funny answer at the ready, effortlessly dealing with any situation. I also wanted to be like that.'* But Jaap could not be James Bond, however much he wanted to. *'As a result, I suffered a lot from fear of failure. Fear and a sense of insecurity cause you to be on the alert at all times. You have your senses wide open and absorb all stimuli around you. You observe everything in an effort to adapt to your surroundings and be able to live up to your ideal image. The result is overstimulation.'*

Jaap now knows how to avoid overstimulation. First and foremost, by learning to understand the world around him. And, equally importantly, by accepting himself as he is. This reduces his level of fear. And if there is still a risk of becoming overexcited, Jaap closes himself off to superfluous stimuli, switching on his 'filters' and concentrating on one thing or person only. *'I don't go to parties that often, but once I'm there, I focus my attention only on the people I'm talking to. I close myself off from whatever else is happening in that room.'* Jaap calls it 'stimulus management'. He thinks that this tool should be further investigated. It may help other people with autism.

The story of Jaap's life is one of trial and error. The latter in particular, though, he has turned into an asset. At the age of four, he was a problem child. In his own words, his behaviour was 'bizarre'. *'You could sit me on your lap, but you would run the risk of me suddenly poking my finger in your eye. Or I would start punching the bellies of people in the swimming pool. I also spat on windows. I lived entirely in a world of my own and was only interested in things, not in people. Kindergarten was not a successful time for me. The teachers had too little time for me, so I was often removed from the group. They would sit me next to a tray of water, or some such thing, which then became the focus of my world.'* His parents tried everything to stimulate his development. The 'Elektro' game, in which you point out two linked objects with the help of two metal pins, causing a light to switch on, was not a success. What he did take to were toddler activities, such as gluing, colouring, painting, cutting out pictures from magazines and making cardboard figures. These activities proved to be so stimulating for his brain that he made an amazing leap in his development between ages four and six. After having carefully looked around for a while, his mother found a place in Amsterdam where he could stay during the day on weekdays. This organisation provided a safe environment where he was closely observed and stimulated in his further development. Jaap is convinced that this place endowed him with the foundation for his ability to handle problems more easily later on in life.

At the age of 11 he was registered with a school for children with a learning difficulties and socio-emotional education problems. It was a difficult time for Jaap. He had to toe the line and was severely bullied — so his memories of the first year are far from pleasant. *'I can remember a project week in which I was constantly bullied,'* he says. *'On the way back from the project week I cried all day.'* In later years, the bullying lessened. He felt more self-confident and commanded respect, thanks to his sturdy build. *'There was a boy I had been afraid of for a long time. Until I dealt him a few blows and discovered that he was actually a wimp. I climbed quite a few steps up the social ladder.'* School was a relatively safe environment for Jaap. There was plenty of structure and it is not a large place. Attending a regular school would probably not have worked out well for Jaap. He could have handled it intellectually, but not socio-emotionally. His mother chose that school on purpose, feeling that if he could succeed there, he would be able to succeed anywhere. It proved to be instrumental in shaping up his mental self-defence. By the end of this period he was a rascal who was a match for the other pupils.

Jaap continued his education at a Montessori secondary school,[1] a pleasant school with 300 pupils. He was shy, especially towards girls, making him an easy target for ridicule

---

1   Montessori education is characterised by an emphasis on independence, freedom within limits, and respect for a child's natural psychological developments.

and badgering. He finished this school and then went on to attend college. *'That was a less pleasant experience, mainly due to the size of the school. It was more of a sort of education factory,'* he says. He describes the problems he encountered there as like being in *'a glass dungeon. I experienced a type of loneliness,'* Jaap explains. *'You feel as if you are covered by a bell jar you take around with you everywhere you go. You can see the world around you, but you cannot touch it. You cannot make contact with other people. You do this to yourself. It is a result of social anxiety, of a sense of insecurity, which in turn is caused by the demands you make on yourself. By high expectations you cannot fulfil. You can eventually break away from this behaviour by changing your expectations and accepting yourself as you are. But this takes time. When you understand the world better, you need not be afraid of it any more and you can accept yourself as you are. You can achieve a great deal, even when you have autism.'*

After college, Jaap goes to study mathematics at Free University in Amsterdam, the Netherlands, and subsequently obtains his doctorate degree at Erasmus University Rotterdam in the same country. *'I have always invested in myself,'* he says. *'That is why I've got this far. I love learning, it makes me feel good. It has often been my ray of hope at times when I did not feel psychologically in order. I wrestled with myself up to the age of 33. I experienced an inner void, loneliness and social anxiety.'* Slowly but surely, however, things started moving in the right direction. After completing his study he went to Ireland to put his research knowledge into practice. He had a good experience there. *'Ireland is not like the Netherlands. People are more easy-going there. I was working at a commercial company and performed well. In my free time I took long walks in the Irish hills and began to develop better socially.'*

At 35, Jaap had the feeling he had cured himself. But at that point, he began to be aware of a new problem: How do I hold on to a job? It took him nine years to understand what was wrong with him and how to deal with it.

After Jaap returned to the Netherlands, he was offered a job at a research institute. *'That turned out to be a real disappointment,'* he sighs. *'The job was too commercial. Being paid by the hour, it just wasn't my thing. I wanted to examine things down to the last detail but there was no time for that. I did have high expectations. My study and my work have always been my pride and that pride was hurt. I did not function well there. I got the feeling that I was just a dumb guy. I could not complete even the simplest of tasks. That was hard to swallow. At the time, I lived in a room of nine square metres, in the house of a very dominant landlady... An unpleasant woman. She wanted to interfere in everything and I had no privacy whatsoever. I sometimes stayed late at work to avoid her.'* He managed to survive for 14 months. *'It was a horrible time. So bad that I even considered suicide.'* It sounds serious, but Jaap never looked for help to overcome his depression, as he believes he himself is responsible for his own happiness. He bought an apartment to get rid of the landlady. This provided him with some relief and the ray of hope he needed. But at work, things did not improve.

He eventually handed in his notice and went in search of a less commercial position, a position he found in America, at a university specialising in bioinformatics. *'America has a rather tough society,'* Jaap says, *'but I still managed to persevere for seven years there and have worked with various employers. The people are friendly but they are very competitive. You really have to prove yourself there.'* His last job in America included working on a data analysis software programme used by biologists from all over the world. The programme consists of 180,000 lines of code. Jaap was given the task of studying the code so that he would be able to work with it independently. But Jaap took his assignment literally, thinking he had to discover the meaning of the entire code in order to be valuable to the company. *'I was expected to be able to start programming after one month, but I just couldn't get round to it as I was still busy figuring out the entire programme. My boss became irritated and a conflict situation arose. Emotions ran high and I wrote a letter about my frustrations to the HR department, in which I went too far. On Monday 14 April at 3.30pm, I had a meeting with the big boss, and at 4.30 I was out of a job. That's the way it works in America.'* Now, years later, Jaap can pinpoint the problem. *'The problem was that I didn't have an overall picture of what my job involved. I should have immersed myself more in the situation. There was no need to master the entire programme. It would have been sufficient to draw up a roadmap of what I had to use to fix the errors quickly. I should have known better as to why I needed to understand the software. I should have communicated better.'*

This is Jaap all over. He is clever enough, on hindsight, to make a good analysis of what went wrong. He rises above himself to create a better version of himself. He does not blame others, even though one could take the view that his superior made mistakes. She did not make herself clear, and could also have communicated better. Jaap shows perseverance. When things get tough, he does not give up. He also has the feeling that things can only get better, as he knows that he can learn from his mistakes. In 2008 he returned to the Netherlands.

The company he now works for in Rotterdam develops diagnostic software for the treatment of acute leukaemia, making use of survival statistics to do so. He very much enjoys working there. But with his current employer as well, there was some uncertainty as to whether he could keep his job. His contract was renewed three times. His employer advised Jaap to have himself assessed for autism, as this would allow for a job coach to be called in to help him with his work. Jaap was placed on the waiting list for assessment on 30 July 2009 but had to wait 11 months for an appointment. Fortunately, his employer did not wait for the diagnosis and gave Jaap a fixed contract. Meanwhile, a few things had changed at work.

The problems with his employer seemed similar to the ones he had in America. At his current job, too, he got entangled in detail. *'I worked myself ragged but we did not make any progress in terms of insight,'* he says. *'I didn't get the job done. I was too focused on details and didn't have an eye for the bigger picture. An issue that has bothered me for years, but one I wasn't able to pinpoint. My supervisor compared me to an ant that covers many kilometres without getting any further. Although I was highly trained, I was unable to use my intelligence to think about the subject matter at a higher level. I was completely chained to the technical details. I wondered: What exactly is this higher level of thought, really? And I came to the conclusion that it simply boiled down to setting targets. When I'm given an assignment now, I don't immediately immerse myself in it. I step back first and ask myself what I want to achieve with the job. What is the underlying goal? But it's not just the goal that matters. Other questions come into play as well. What will happen to my work? Who will do something with the results, and how can I best be of use to them?'*

Jaap eventually discovered that he needed to make connections: his work is not a separate matter but is connected to a larger whole. It was this insight that helped him move on. *'Connecting also meant that I had to communicate more. I simply cannot always work out everything by myself, even though I have tried for a long time. So the next step is asking for feedback. I finally started communicating about my work. Very specifically. This creates structure in my work.'* The person to whom Jaap can talk about his work does have to meet certain conditions, though, to have a proper understanding of how Jaap thinks and what he finds difficult. Jaap is lucky to have someone like that in the company. Someone who empathises with him and with whom he can talk. Jaap now manages to identify targets and structure his work, and to make the proper connections himself. He no longer chooses the hard way and does no more than necessary to achieve the set goal. Regular consultation prevents him from getting lost in details that do not matter.

Apart from setting goals and communicating better, Jaap has made another important choice which improves his work considerably. *'I know where my strength lies and have decided to use it more in my work. I am incredibly good at technical documentation. I can unravel very complex problems and present them in easily manageable chunks for people to understand. I get a lot of recognition for it, but I am also good at analysing and have made an important contribution to the continuation of a company product. If that had not worked out, it would have cost the company a lot of money. A very important reason for my improved performance is becoming more self-confident. I am no longer a plaything of my emotions. I have risen above my autism by becoming very self-aware. I do not have the luxury of functioning on autopilot like other people. I have built that pilot myself. I think carefully about everything I do. It does take more energy but it is very rewarding.'*

Jaap regards high-functioning autism as a form of genius. People with autism can concentrate very well on a problem and continue thinking and puzzling until the problem is solved. But how many people still get enough time to solve problems in our current society? Everything has to be quick and goal-oriented these days. Jaap uses his genius to adapt to that fast-moving society, and with success. In so doing he refutes the opinion of his co-promoter, who once told him that he was best suited to solving complex problems on his own in a quiet room. Jaap did not take this as a compliment, and the remark motivated him enormously. He wanted to prove his co-promoter wrong.

Jaap has worked in Ireland and America, has played rugby, has celebrated carnival dressed up as a woman and has moved house many times in his life. People with autism do not like parties and changes at all. People with autism do not like networking either. But Jaap has done so, and has done so expressly for a better chance on the labour market. He has managed to bring his doctorate to the attention of people all over the world. This eventually resulted in his job in America. Jaap calls it *'possibility thinking'*, thinking in opportunities. He laughingly calls himself *'an adventurous autistic person'*.

Jaap now has a permanent contract and works full-time. And that is very important. It has enabled him to buy a house of his own. He had fallen in love with the house but managed to wait for a long time before finally purchasing it, waiting for the price to drop considerably. He was able to resist the temptation to go ahead with the deal earlier, which is remarkable when you consider that he was sleeping in a hostel at the time. He kept this up for five months. *'And that's no picnic for someone with autism,'* he says. *'I slept with seven adolescents in a dorm. I had to share a shower with seven other people, and now I have two showers all to myself.'* The security he now has is a victory. A nice permanent job and a house. The appreciation of his colleagues and his employer. These are important factors for happiness. For a very long time, Jaap felt like an 'underdog' but that time has passed. He is proud of what he has achieved. *'This really is as good as it gets,'* he says. But then again? Now he just needs to find a wife, but he is working on that.

AIRPLANE

Jaap gives lectures to autistic people, care providers, parents of autistic children and other interested parties. He tells the story of his life and shares his view on how best to handle overstimulation and autism. The reactions to his lectures are mostly positive, but he does sometimes have to deal with disappointment. He was recently told at a lecture that it was easy for him to talk as he was blessed with favourable conditions, such as strong parental support, high intelligence and perseverance. A completely unjust remark, Jaap thinks. *'That would mean that you have an excuse not to become successful if you do not have those favourable conditions. That answer puts paid to any further discussion.'* We apparently find it easier to hide behind disadvantage than to look at whatever is in our favour. Jaap is an example of how far you can go, provided you work hard enough at overcoming your own weaknesses. He has not opted for the easy way. He has invented himself very consciously; first emotionally and cognitively, later professionally as well. *'Maybe I can provide an analogy,'* Jaap says. *'Most people are given a completely finished airplane at birth. They only have to learn how to fly. People with autism do not get an airplane but a kit for making one themselves. In order to be able to fly just like others, they first have to unwrap and assemble the kit.'*

2.

THE WOMAN WHO
FENDS FOR HERSELF

Wendy Vinck (37) is a teacher for children with severe behavioural and/or socio-emotional problems in Belgium. She has known since 2004 that she has autism. She is highly gifted.

At the end of March 2011, Wendy Vinck is a guest at the Belgian television programme 'The Latest Show' on the occasion of World Autism Day. Before Wendy enters, presenter Michiel Devlieger asks the people in the audience not to applaud. Instead, they can wave. The audience waves and Wendy steps up and shakes hands with Michiel. She explains: '*I cannot tolerate sudden sounds or sounds that do not have any structure, without a clearly defined start and finish.*' Appearing on television does not make her nervous. She has prepared herself well and knows exactly what is going to happen. She answers the questions quick-wittedly, almost as if she is a weekly guest on the show. She explains perfectly how someone with autism thinks and feels. The audience is quiet.

'My doorbell does not work but I will keep an eye on the door,' she emails in advance. The moment we approach the door, we hear a buzzer and the door unlocks. We can go in. Later, she says that she has disabled the doorbell herself; she considers the doorbell to be a nuisance. Wendy is not very fond of unannounced visitors or strangers at the door. On several occasions people have called for reasons she did not properly understand. For example, people from the waste collection department who came to wish her a happy New Year. They wanted a tip, of course, but they did not explain that. Wendy was just supposed to know. But for her, the matter was not self-evident. She politely wished them a happy New Year in return and left it at that. She was blind to the context according to which people without autism could infer that these men had called with an unspoken purpose. Wendy is now aware of the matter and it will not happen to her a second time. All the more because the doorbell has been disabled. People now come by only when announced, and send her a text message when they are at the door. That said, people actually rarely or never call at her house. Furthermore, when someone calls her on the telephone and she does not recognise the number, she does not answer. *'If it is important, people will leave a voicemail message,'* she says. But she does not often return the call. Only if it is really important. This works well for Wendy.

Wendy was diagnosed in 2004 but she had had professional counselling a few times before. *'From tutoring and therapy to reduce fear of failure to psychological help,'* she says. *'Especially when I was still attending high school and during the transition to tertiary education. But autism was never considered. In 2003, I went to live on my own and changed jobs. That was when things went totally wrong. A lot of structure was gone, there were too many changes in a short space of time, I had a lot of free time that I suddenly had to fill myself… I did not eat. I did not sleep. I had totally lost my day and night rhythm. I was care coordinator at a school. When I came home, I continued working on tasks I was busy with and I continued until I had to go to work again in the morning. I eventually set the alarm clock to go to sleep. I noticed that I had a problem, from the reactions of people around me as well. But I did not panic. In order to be helped quickly, admission into a psychiatric hospital was the only option. I finally wanted to know what was the matter with me. I was hospitalised for two weeks. Then I myself chose to call in ambulatory care, a number of short treatments sessions, that after each session I could return home. I was referred to the psychiatrist I still see even now. The suspicion slowly arose that I might be autistic. After tests and discussions with a multidisciplinary team the suspicion was confirmed. Six months later I was diagnosed.'* It proved to be difficult to diagnose Wendy correctly. She thinks she knows the reason. *'As years go by, you get better and better at camouflaging and compensating for the external behavioural characteristics of autism. You make the impression of functioning normally by cognitively compensating for what you do not sense or know intuitively due to your autistic way of thinking.'*

Prior to that difficult period, Wendy lived with her parents where she did notice that she was different from others. She has a sister who is two years her junior. *'Everything went relatively well until my sister started to develop an interest in boys. Then my anchor disappeared. Then, too, I noticed that things worked differently for me. I did not care much for boys. A lot of it makes sense to me now that I have been diagnosed. Arguments, misunderstandings and things I had to do but did not understand why. When something changed, I became very annoying. I could not handle it well. I remember that when I was a toddler, my father always gave me a matchbox car in the paper shop. When I went to the shop with my mother one time, I didn't get a car. I raised hell in the shop because I always got one.'*

Her mother was the financial director of a number of companies, her father was a chemist. In a chemist, a touch of autism could be suspected. Wendy actually thinks that her father might well be autistic, too. *'If he would let himself be tested, I think there is a good chance. But my parents are not concerned about it at all. They have never talked about my diagnosis. I do talk about it, but they do not respond. It is a pity, really, as it might certainly clarify a number of things. It would help explain why I make so many mistakes without noticing.'*

At school Wendy was bullied a lot, causing her to switch primary schools. But at her new school, too, she was bullied, which convinced the people around her that the fault lay with her. In the third year at secondary school she started having problems with tests. She blanked, even though she actually knew the subject matter well. She was given support by a centre for student supervision.

She went on to study architecture. *'While I chose that,'* she says, *'I actually did not really know what I wanted to do. The only thing I knew was that I did not want to work in an office. I wanted to do something creative. And as I was really good at mathematics and scientific drawing, that seemed a good choice.'* Wendy did follow the years of training to become an architect, but when her sister started teacher training, she discovered that she thought that job was much more interesting. *'When I looked more deeply into my sister's training course, I thought: maybe this will allow me to understand how people think. I did not understand what kept students and young adults so interested. Going to student parties, skipping classes, changing boyfriends and girlfriends all the time... I didn't understand why they did all that and why they interacted like that. I did not connect with them either, unless it was to serve as a taxi driver for my sister and her boyfriends and girlfriends, ferrying them to and from parties. I suddenly started to realise this, at that age. I hoped the training would help me to understand all this better, and to learn how to behave "normally". I learned a lot from the lessons on communication.'*

Wendy mentions 'Leary's Rose', a communication model that is derived from psychological research into the effect of behaviour. The Rose of Leary assumes that behaviour creates behaviour; of action and reaction, cause and effect, sending and receiving. The Rose of Leary would show what behaviour is evoked by certain behaviour and how to influence behaviour. The theory has been developed by (among others) Timothy Leary. In this manner patterns of behaviour can be analysed and one's own behaviour can be used in order to influence.

Wendy also mentions Ferdinand Cuvelier's rose of axes, a model for identifying characteristics of interaction between people. This model provides us with language to talk about the way people interact. Using this theory we can take a critical view of our own behaviour and the effects of this behaviour on others, thus improving interaction with others. The model is based on Leary's Rose. The difference between the two models lies in the fact that Leary's Rose is based on a person's behaviour in relation to the behaviour of another person. The rose of axes, or relationship rose, is based – in contrast – on a person's attitude towards another person.

Schools work with the rose of axes to teach children social skills; as it happened, so did the first school where Wendy worked. We can well imagine how useful these scientific tools are for people with autism, who have difficulty understanding personal interaction. *'At the time, I did not yet know that I had autism, but I found it a useful system to learn to communicate with people. It has helped me to understand interactions. I started to grasp why people say something the moment they are about to say something. For example, because they are angry. I have learned to respond effectively to that. Prior to learning this, I always handled all this the wrong way. I reacted too directly and too honestly. I still am honest, but I will respond in a more appropriate manner, something I could not do before. When people got angry with me, even though I thought I was simply being honest and direct, I became angry as well. I couldn't understand what I was doing wrong.'*

Wendy did not make many friends, as a result. She still does not have any friends, she says. *'In order to get to know people well and "learn them by heart", I need to see them very often, otherwise they become too unpredictable for me. And I belong to an age category in which all those people have families, so they do not have time to see me regularly.'* And how about colleagues? *'At the first school I worked for, I did undertake things with colleagues outside school hours. Initially, we spent a lot of time together elaborating project activities, and this sometimes led to us going for a drink, on the occasion of a birthday or something like that. So, at that moment, I considered them to be friends. I still see them occasionally but I do not call them friends any more. They have become strangers to me. That is very difficult to explain. For normal people apparently it is possible to have someone continue to be a friend, even if you only see that person sporadically.*

That is strange to me. I have little to no contact outside school hours with the colleagues I now work with. So it's really not possible to build up a friendship.'

Are there no people Wendy can turn to when necessary? She does not take long to answer: *'Myself. I always try to solve things myself.'* And this works out all right? *'More or less.'* And what if it does not? *'If possible, I leave things as they are.'* Not too positive an answer. We ask if Wendy is happy at all. *'What is happiness? I cannot imagine things any other way. I need to be at peace with the way things are now. Some days, I do not like it at all that I am lonely, have no companion, no one to turn to. But there are also days when I don't have a problem with all this at all, and am relieved that I don't continually have to take someone else into consideration.'* The key question here is, of course, whether Wendy would like things to be different. *'Of course I'd prefer to be normal. No doubt in my mind. I certainly notice that my disability restricts me in very many things. I do often feel frustrated, as I can only to a limited extent, if at all, do or show what I know and feel inside. I continually need to think hard about how I live, because my autism makes me blind to any context I am faced with and I need to specifically consider that context again and again.'*

The diagnosis came as a relief to Wendy. *'It finally became clear that I didn't act as I did, and do, on purpose. And it allows me to look at myself in a more focused manner. Look at why things don't work. I happened to have just started a course on autism for my advanced teacher training for special education. I had realised that what I read there about autism was like a description of the way I was. So the diagnosis was actually no surprise. Thanks to being diagnosed, I got to recognise pitfalls and know my limitations better.'* One of the things Wendy learned about herself is that she cannot handle the unexpected well – though, to be fair, this is not always the case. If something unexpected happens at her work, this is usually no problem. She always has some alternative scenario she can use in reserve. Apart from being a special education teacher, she also teaches at higher education institutions. There, she was once faced with having to teach a group of students five times larger than she had anticipated. She had to switch to a larger lecture hall at the last moment. *'With a reader and a microphone. There were 108 students. I did need to get myself together and quickly think of a solution, which different work and organisation methods to deploy all of a sudden. But I still had a supervisory role and was teaching a subject I knew. But if I'm not the one in charge and simply have to take what comes, I find it much more difficult if things suddenly change in such a way that I need to take action. Suppose I went to a musical and they called out from the stage that the person in seat so-and-so — my seat — had won a prize…I would freeze.'* So you won't make Wendy happy by organising a surprise party for her. Most people like getting presents, but Wendy finds even the thought abhorrent.

Wendy does not like change in the supermarket either. If she is used to buying a certain brand of rice, she only ever wants that rice. If that brand is no longer on the shelves, she goes to other supermarkets looking for her familiar rice, instead of switching to another brand. *'I used to really panic if a certain brand was no longer sold. Fortunately, this reaction has waned. I have learned to control myself and not make a fool of myself on the spot. My medication helps as well. But when I get home, I do need to recover for a little while. Sometimes, when my coping strategies have been overtaxed and I have run out, I can still freeze and be unable to utter a word of sense. I start stuttering and am simply rooted to the spot.'*

Wendy is a special education teacher. A certain number of her pupils also have ASD. Does she understand these children better than a 'normal' school teacher would? *'I have always understood these pupils better. But at first, it did trouble me. It wasn't so much a problem for me, but what about the children? Was that really a good idea, having a teacher with a disability teach a class of children with a disability? I can teach them all kinds of things they need, but it is hard to teach things that you are not familiar with yourself. Or so I thought at first. I now am 100 per cent sure that it is an advantage for me, and also for the children. My use of language is always suitably adapted to them. I do not need to think consciously about speaking in a very concrete and clear manner. I can be myself. I understand them better if they do not want to do something or find it pointless. As a child I found reading comprehension stupid, for example. Having to answer questions, the answers to which can simply be found in the text was silly. The teacher is quite capable of reading that text himself, after all, I thought as a child. So I try to avoid doing this in my class, because it's really stupid. It's not functional. When I teach reading comprehension, for example, I provide them with a game and they have to read the rules of the game. If they don't understand them, they can't play the game. At least there is some purpose in it then. Another issue. I teach children with behavioural problems. I understand that the behavioural problem is often a result of frustration and not of evil intent. And I do not take anything personally. Sometimes, colleagues are called names by pupils. Those colleagues find this difficult and feel attacked. I don't. I think: that student has a hard time and I happen to be conveniently around to call names at. This is not to say that I approve of it, but I do not feel attacked as a person.'*

Wendy also observes differently from her colleagues, she explains. Sometimes teachers have to observe a child and write down what the child does. When a child holds a pen in their hand and keeps pressing the cap, Wendy writes it down like that, while a colleague would write that the child was playing with a pen. That is a substantial difference. Wendy's work is very meaningful, no doubt about it. But does it give her satisfaction? *'It is meaningful to the children and the parents. They are happy when they see their child making progress. But satisfaction for me? It is simply my job. And to get satisfaction from my job I need to get sufficient "nourishment" to satisfy my "mental appetite". When a child completely deadlocks in a certain way, it is a challenge for me to investigate and discover points of entry to help develop that child. When I then see that it works, the challenge is gone.'*

'The behaviour of people with autism is certainly not the standard,' Wendy says when we talk about what is normal and what is not. *'But that is not caused by their behaviour, but because they think*

differently. That is very difficult to explain.' It becomes painful when this leads to lack of understanding. Strange and avoidable problems can arise for people with autism when neurotypicals have no idea whatsoever what having autism entails. Wendy has experienced this herself in public transport. An example. One day, at 11pm, she needed to travel home from Gent (Belgium). Her travel card had run out of credit. No problem, as there are ticket machines everywhere. But these turned out to be out of order. She got in the tram and walked up to the conductor. However, they are not allowed to sell tickets any more. She explained the situation. The guard advised her to get off at the next stop and buy a ticket there. But Wendy did not want to, as it was already late and she did not like the idea of standing alone on a deserted platform where she normally never gets off. She did not know what to do and stayed sitting in the tram. *'I was under a lot of stress at that moment as I had not paid. But the guard did not want to sell me a ticket, whereas I did have the money.'* Just before she had to get off, an inspector came. She explained the situation and said that the conductor did not want to sell her a ticket. The ticket inspector went up to the conductor to check her story, but the conductor denied it. She was issued a fine not only for fare-dodging but also for disrespect, because she said that the conductor was lying. Later she emailed the transport company, explaining that her autism plays up in that type of situation. But it had no effect whatsoever. No understanding from the transport company. Antwerp (Belgium) clearly does not (yet) have autism-friendly public transport.

Does having autism also give Wendy any advantages? She thinks for a long time before answering. *'When I do something I want to do it perfectly. I really dive into what I do and want to know everything. I hate being faced with surprises. I dare say that I know more about pedagogical and didactic aspects of education than the average teacher, maybe even head master. When people from the Ministry of Education come for inspection, like this school year, I look up their favourite topics and specialisations. I want to know them beforehand. I am well prepared then. I know what subjects I had better discuss or not. But I doubt if many ordinary people consider that an advantage. They may think that is too much work.'*

She has learned by now to do things other than work outside school hours. But when she says what those things are, we raise our eyebrows, as they are not exactly relaxing activities. She says that, apart from working at her own school, she teaches students on two teacher-training courses, provides education to teachers who want to gain more in-depth knowledge of a topic, and gives refresher courses in other schools. And that she is helping to develop a new method of language teaching. She took courses up until last year, but by now she has completed all the teacher-training courses she can do after school hours. *'I have recently found something enabling me to get back to school: a new, three-year advanced school development course. Another possibility to nurture my mind a little, another challenge, some more free time that I can spend in contact with others.'*

'The disadvantage of working in education is that you have a lot of holidays,' Wendy says. We laugh. We believe most teachers consider this to be a big advantage. But not Wendy. For years, she would spend her holidays working as a supervisor on holidays for mentally handicapped adults. She did this together with a former colleague. Some time ago, however, the latter got married and that brought an end to the voluntary work activities for the two of them. *'I would never do that with a total stranger,'* Wendy says. It would be too stressful for her. The last few years Wendy has spent much of her holidays cycling. *'I really had to learn that, because I thought riding a bike without going anywhere in particular was silly. But with the multi-stop bicycle route system I can set up a bicycle route beforehand, look up the sights along the way and read a little about them.'* Sometimes, when she has too much on her mind, she sits at the table and does a jigsaw puzzle. *'I have discovered by chance that that is the only way not to worry.'*

Wendy has ambitions, but her autism impedes her ability to realise them. She would, for example, like to teach more at colleges, or supervise children with learning and/ or developmental disorders, but this requires a great many arrangements. In the administrative sense, for example. *'I would love to work more hours at college, or as supervisor of children with autism, and less as a class teacher in special education. There are still challenges for me in that area. But I cannot get there yet, as it will entail steps I cannot or dare not take. I don't know what I need to do, exactly, or whom I need to address. I cannot think ahead while I am really busy with my regular work today. I work full-time and cannot focus on two things at once. That is very frustrating.'* Wendy could actually do with some form of support to develop her talents further. A coach. But, again, she is assertive. She knows she has to solve her own problems, and that she is able to. She plans to take action in the coming summer holidays. She rather likes the idea of a coach. *'A sort of help line you can call just when you need to at that moment.'*

A last question for Wendy. Does she believe she is well enough to be herself? *'Here at home, always,'* she answers. And the minute she mingles with people? *'Never. I always have to adapt. Unless it specifically concerns activities for adults with autism.'* Can she think of a society in which she could always be herself? *'That is utopia. Apparently a lot of energy is required for neurotypicals to interact with people with autism. I even notice this at my work. And then you are talking about teachers who teach in special education. When they are too busy or do not feel happy, they have difficulty dealing with me. It demands too much effort. At such times, being understanding is difficult enough, let alone adapting. I would be quite content if some understanding were shown. I don't ask for adaptations, although I can think of some. For example, clearer and unambiguous communication. But gradually I am seeing improvements. Some years ago, for example, I got into trouble because I had not completed the attendance register. I know it sounds stupid, but I always have to do that with the same type of pen, which I had forgotten to bring. So I had not completed it. That excuse was not accepted. It was a stupid one in their view. Now, they would be more understanding. By this time I have such a pen both at home and at school, so this situation doesn't arise any more. But, in the end, I myself have chosen to function in this society. This also implies having chosen to make an effort. The only thing I hope is that people understand how it works for someone with autism. I would be quite happy with that.'*

3.

'WE WANT JOBS'

Nita Jackson (29) and **Drew Miles** (29) both have Asperger's and are 'unemployed'.

'I'm regarded as a" freak" by most people,' Nita Jackson wrote in her book *Standing Down Falling Up: Asperger's syndrome from the Inside Out* (2001).[1] *'Firstly because I like wearing luminous clothing in the daytime, use goggles as a hair accessory, and often spray my hair bright yellow, pink or blue; secondly because basically I'm just B-ZAR!! I'm an eccentric as well as an Aspee…'* She wrote the book when she was 17, and from her website nitajackson.com we learn that she has also had two plays performed. She speaks at conferences about her autism and other 'disabilities' and by the time this book is published, her second book will be available in the bookshops. Our conclusion was a given: we had to interview her, as we might learn a lot. And we did. Not only from her, but also from her friend Drew Miles, whom she brought with her.

When we meet we are all a little bit stressed. Nita told us on the phone that she was waiting for us in a Starbucks coffee corner, but there are more than one of those in Liverpool Street Station. When we finally find each other, Drew is running up and down looking for us, and Nita has her phone to her ear, telling me that she is the one standing up. Nevertheless, after a few minutes we are all comfortable with our drinks and Drew

---

1   Jackson, N. (2002) *Standing Down – Falling Up: Asperger's Syndrome from the Inside Out.* London: Sage Publications Ltd.

and Nita are telling us all we want to know about the impact of Asperger's syndrome on their lives.

Drew and Nita met in 2000 at the launch of a training video they had both participated in. The video was for school staff, parents and pupils, to explain what it meant to have ASD. Nita and Drew were interviewed. *'There was only a basic interpretation of what autism was in those days,'* Nita explains.

By that time they both had difficult years behind them. Drew was 14 when he was diagnosed with Asperger's in 1998. *'There was a lot of bullying at school,'* he tells us. *'It affected me so much that I started with anti-depressants after counselling. The consequence was that I felt like a different person, brain chemistry doesn't work when you have Asperger's. When I lowered the dose of anti-depressants, I began to feel more anxious and depressed in school. I started to show very clear suicidal tendencies. This was a turning point; my parents realised we had to go a step further. A few months later I was diagnosed with Asperger's. The interesting thing with me is that, because I have overcome some typical issues of Asperger's, like understanding social concepts and displaying social skills, I give the impression now of not having it at all.'*

Drew tried to understand his Asperger's through experience, while his parents tried to do so by reading books about autism. That's why his mother got a very black-and-white view of what Asperger's is. Drew: *'Some people think that there is a mild form of Asperger's, but there isn't. It is a big puzzle and some of the pieces are missing. And for every person with Asperger's, different pieces are missing. It's never the same and not that easy. I had problems with adolescent social skills. At that time I was not good at making eye contact, for instance. I was shy. When I began to socialise with one particular group of people, a fringe group, you could say, my social skills improved a lot. In a matter of months, I turned myself into a social butterfly. At the same time there was a domestic conflict going on. My family didn't approve of the alternative lifestyle I was adopting. I was 17 at that time. My parents believed that I was getting involved in something that was much more sleazy than it actually was.'* The fact that, in the same period, Drew made it clear that he was gay, didn't help to restore the relationship with his parents. In their view, he could never live a happy life as a gay man because of his Asperger's.

Nita was 15 when she was diagnosed with Asperger's. On her website we can read that a short time before she was diagnosed, her parents wanted to put her in mental hospital. We are relieved to hear her say that this was a joke, but nevertheless it was not very far from the truth. *'Actually, they thought that I was mad,'* explains Nita. *'My parents did, and so did the teachers at the four schools I went to. I left three schools because I was extremely bullied. I was known as a very odd child. I never walked normally, but in an autistic way, as if I was falling over. And if I was spoken to, I didn't make eye contact, and I had an odd manner of speech. In an attempt to socialise, I learned scripts to repeat in a mechanical way. I always had my head down, and if I had to talk about something it was about things I was obsessed with at the time. It was pretty obvious that I was a very odd and abnormal child. And that was what everybody called me, even my parents. It was never neutral, it was always negative. A lot of people in my family still avoid talking to me.'*

We can imagine what this does to a child's self-confidence. Nita: *'At first, I seemed to be OK with it, but suddenly things got on top of me. My self-confidence hit rock bottom and everything terrified me. If I put on the television and something happened in a programme I was watching, even if it was a cartoon, I would be mortified. If things were not absolutely in order, or different from the day before, I panicked. Everything that could panic me, would panic me. You can say that I tried to avoid life.'*

Her parents had known from the day she was born that she was a 'different' child. Nita: *'My parents went to a score of doctors, paediatricians and psychiatrists to find out what was "wrong" with me. And "wrong" is the word they use. Finally, when I was 14, my mother found out about Asperger's syndrome. We went to a local paediatrician whom I had never met before, and he thought that I was a classic case – as far as women go, he told us, because with women the symptoms are more subtle. I don't know what he meant, because mine weren't subtle at all.'*

Nita is 29-years-old now and there is not much left of the shy girl she once was. She doesn't talk mechanically, it's pleasant to listen to her. She makes jokes and laughs and speaks about herself with confidence. She speaks at conferences about Asperger's and writes books about her life. We wonder what happened to her in the last ten years. *'I don't know, the change came gradually, I think. When I left high school I was this tiny, introverted mouse of a person, with strange outbursts of activity. I also have ADD* (attention deficit disorder). *So, normally, I would run around screaming a lot and waving my hands about, and then suddenly I would realise that I needed to go and hide myself. Occasionally this may still happen, when I am very stressed for instance.'*

Nita studied English language and literature, music and business studies. The sad thing is that she cannot find a proper job. *'For a long time I have wanted to start a career in translating and interpreting. I am qualified for that. However, putting autism syndrome on my CV seems to land my application right in the bin. I have filled in hundreds of application forms, and have even got help from a professional CV company.'* We tell Nita and Drew that Belgium and the Netherlands have job agencies that specialise in helping people with Asperger's. And people with ASD have special qualities. *'Autism specialist employment agencies do exist,'* Nita says, *'but, like any other agency in England they are quite restricted in what they can offer.'* So Nita had no choice but to start her own business. A problem is that Nita is also discalculate, dyslectic and apraxic. This didn't stop her from setting up her own nail art studio and website – further proof of her creativity and perseverance.

Drew graduated third class from a university course in philosophy and politics. After graduating he tried to find employment, but he wasn't successful either. In 2004 he was living with a seriously disabled friend, caring for him as far as possible. *'I was the only person who could help him. Because he trusted and valued me so much, he took me on as a paid carer, but this only lasted for a month. He became ill and died. After that I suffered from anxiety and depression. Especially because of my friend's death, and other things that had an impact around that time. It all made me paranoid and I thought that I was meant to die. But instead of me, it was my dad who died in the summer of 2005. My mother married an old friend. So I am part of a broader family now, in which I am the odd one out, the black sheep. Also because I am still single and unemployed.'*

Like Nita, at the age of 29 he is *'trying to deal with life'*. Maybe now even more than he had to in his childhood. In the last eight years, psychiatrists have wanted to treat him for depression. Drew: *'I am depressed, but anxiety is causing it. And I believe this is the case for a lot of people on the spectrum. Psychiatrists tend to think that depression is causing the anxiety but it is the anxiety, that causes the depression. So I focus on the anxiety.'*

Drew is occasionally asked to perform as an entertainer. With a small change of hairstyle he looks exactly like Boris Johnson, Mayor of London and British Conservative Party politician. He got paid gigs for the *Sunday Times* and even the Police Federation, who wanted him to show up as Boris Johnson at the Conservative Party Conference in Birmingham. Drew: *'There are prospects for me in this direction, I think. I have brief moments in the sun now, although I don't think much has changed in the last eight years as far as having a career is concerned. I am sad about the fact that I didn't have the advantage of graduating young. I could have been an asset to the right people, but the way the job market works is so bad that it didn't get me anywhere. Like many other people on the spectrum, I don't have much confidence that this will change.'*

For Nita it is the same story. She tries not to think about her future too much, as it appears rather bleak to her. *'For the last eight years I haven't even been anywhere near to finding work. It's a two-way street. It is not only us – the people on the spectrum – who need to change. The way the system works has to change as well. If you are not a supremely self-confident, go-getting and determined type of person, then there is no room for you. The job market system in England is unfriendly for people on the autism spectrum. I have got friends with Asperger's who have jobs, but they are very good at concealing it. And they never disclosed it on their CVs. While people like Drew and I – who mention it – got turned down.'* Drew: *'And at the same time they consider us to be workshy. But it's not our choice to depend on the state.'* Nita: *'We want jobs.'*

Nita calls herself an advocate for people with Asperger's. She speaks at conferences, for instance, about what it is like for women to have Asperger's. Drew also has ideas for projects to raise awareness about Asperger's, but he cannot find the drive to get them off the ground. He laughs, points his finger at Nita and says: *'But it will be all right, I am dragged into her orbit.'* They might even write a book together. We think they should. Maybe they can change things and make the world a little better for people on the autism spectrum.

4.

'WE NEED TO EXPLAIN TO EMPLOYERS WHERE PROFIT CAN BE MADE'

Annelies Spek, clinical psychologist and senior scientific researcher at the Autism Centre for Adults in the Netherlands.

Annelies Spek carries out diagnostic research involving adults with a possible ASD. In 2010 she obtained her doctorate at Leiden University (the Netherlands). The subject of her thesis focuses on the strengths and weaknesses of adults with autism. She gives postgraduate courses on autism to psychologists and psychiatrists and has developed the successful '*mindfulness*' training for adults with autism. What reason more do we want to have a talk with Annelies? An enthusiastic expert has the floor.

Before we have asked a single question, we are already engaged in animated discussion. Autism as a quality. Is that possible? Annelies mentions the example of a pathology lab assistant with autism who had to assess medical imagery for evidence of prostate cancer, and was able to identify twice as many cases as an average colleague. This is not to say that autism makes the difference, but it may well be possible. Annelies says that line managers with autism may also have an advantage. '*A line manager must not think from emotional and social conditions,*' Annelies says. '*He must be able to say: "There are too many people here and a few need to go!" That is very analytical. Then, autism can be quite handy.'* Annelies sees people with autism at all levels, including more important positions: *'Directors of schools and companies, for example. It is often said that people with autism cannot be managers, but that is not true. They often have strong analytical skills and are able to analyse companies in detail. And as they do not take the social approach so much, this sometimes enables them to take harder measures, in particular.'*

We leave it at that for the time being and return to the qualities and the limitations of people with autism later on in the interview. First, we want to know why Annelies, as a psychologist, has specialised in autism. *'Because people with autism are so real,'* she says. *'What you see is what you get. They will never manipulate, they are very pure, and I enjoy that very much. I also like the humour and the language jokes. They sometimes make strange and unexpected associations.'* An example of a typical autism joke? *'During one mindfulness training, a trainer explained the concept of a mantra: "If you feel a bit out of sorts, concentrate on a certain word and repeat it to yourself." A man in the group said he preferred concentrating on an image instead of a word, laughing as he sketched the outline of a woman with his hands. At which point another man spontaneously called out: "Oh, that's not a mantra but a womantra!"* People sometimes say that individuals with autism don't have a sense of humour, but that is not true.

Let's talk about other, more serious matters now. We have read that the distinction between Asperger's syndrome and autism will probably no longer be used. Why is that? *'That is right. There is not enough evidence that it concerns two different syndromes. We have, however, always made the distinction. In the case of Asperger's, some characteristics are excessively present. They make frequent eye contact or stare a lot, talk profusely and have a vivid imagination. In addition, they are somewhat clumsy in motor skills. However, their language development is not delayed, and people with Asperger's all have average to high intelligence. In the case of autism, it is more a matter of too little eye contact, communication and imagination. Motor skills are often somewhat stiff. Nevertheless, for the most part there is little difference between high-level autism and Asperger's. In America extensive research has been carried out which showed that the city where someone had been diagnosed was one of the main factors that determined whether they were diagnosed with autism or Asperger's. In addition, we regularly see people with characteristics of both autism and Asperger's, like displaying a lot of eye contact but little in the way of conversation, a broad imagination but stiff motor skills, and so on – cases that could nominally be designated half autism and half Asperger's. So in practice the distinction between autism and Asperger's does not work well. The result is that our organisation no longer provides a distinct Asperger's syndrome diagnosis.'*

If there is such a wide range in the manifestation of autism, you might suppose that there are many people walking around who function perfectly well with ASD and have never been diagnosed. Everybody knows people in their environment who are suspected to be autistic. *'Someone with autism can, in a very structured environment in which it is clear what is expected of him or her, also at social level, function extremely well,'* Annelies says. *'A disorder is only diagnosed the moment inconvenience is experienced, be it that the persons in question are troubled themselves, or that the people near to them are. Now depression, for instance, is something that always causes suffering, and therefore clearly is a disorder. In the case of autism one can ask oneself whether it is a disorder, or a way of processing information that typically leads to you having little rapport with your environment. People are now diagnosed with autism more frequently, possibly because they break down sooner in our present society than they did in the past. This may be related to the fact that we have created a much more socially involving education system. Everybody has to work in groups, even at the technical universities. Cooperating is often difficult for people with autism. That causes people with autism to get into trouble and break down sooner nowadays. Many children with ASD now end up in the special education system. This is a good thing on the face of it, as they get more attention. On the other hand, it may also be stigmatising. And it is sometimes very important for children with autism to have contact with ordinary children. And conversely, for ordinary children to have contact with children who are different.'*

So we have to conclude that our way of organising society, our education system, our work and our usual manners more or less excludes and troubles an entire group of people with common characteristics – to the extent that they need to be diagnosed with 'a defect' that did not exist in the past. Annelies has a clear opinion on the matter: *'Assistance provided to people with autism should not revolve around the question of how to make them "better" but, on the contrary, around how to ensure that they can express themselves and make use of their talents. And in addition, around how to ensure that they experience as little trouble as possible around what makes them different from other people in society.'* Do we still need to talk about a disorder, then? *'In order to be able to provide counselling to someone, we unfortunately have to demonstrate that the person concerned has a disorder. But if the majority of people in society had autism, that society would be very different. Then we would be the ones breaking down.'*

The crux is to establish the qualities of people with autism. If you do that, it may already be enough to help them with minor adaptations in their daily lives. *'For us, a break is relaxing,'* Annelies says, *'but for someone with autism it often isn't, because he or she will then have to chitchat with colleagues. But if that person goes outside for a walk and their colleagues realise they feel better doing this, a lot has been solved already.'* Consider Carlo Post (see Chapter 16), who told us that at work he can sit in the far corner of the open-plan office, listening to classical music on his headphones. Explaining the matter to colleagues is, then, half the battle: making people in the environment of the person with autism aware of the matter, and thereby making that person feel more secure. They must be allowed to be who they are. The employer plays a part in this and needs to make additional efforts. There lies a problem, according to Annelies, as every adjustment in a company, including paying special attention to employees with autism, costs time and money. But there is hope. *'There*

are companies who train people with autism for specific positions,'
Annelies says. *'In Philips' employment creation plan, people with
autism are trained to become testers of hardware and software,
procedures and manuals. If there is one thing they are good at, it is
working with detail. They are much better at this than most people
without autism will ever be. If they do a good job and feel at ease doing
it, employers can benefit for a long time from these people. People with
autism do not like change. The once-only investment needed to train
them is repaid with interest.'*

What about people with ASD who look for help at the
organisation where Annelies works, the Autism Centre? Do
they have work? *'It is difficult for people with autism to find suitable
work,'* Annelies says. *'But a large proportion of the people we see
here have a job. Nevertheless, they experience problems at work sooner
than people without autism. There are several reasons why they can get
into trouble. One important reason is that they are overstimulated – for
example, due to environmental noise. This easily overburdens them. It
may also happen that they are given insufficient structure and clarity.
In that case, they do not know what to do, which causes a lot of stress.
This can be the consequence of a reorganisation, for example. People
with autism cannot handle changes related to reorganisations well.
Sometimes, there are also problems in the social field, conflicts they
cannot handle. They don't understand the signals of other people well,
or are themselves not properly understood by other people. Someone
with autism, for example, does not hesitate to tell his boss that he or
she is not doing a good job. They can't tell that the average boss doesn't
appreciate being criticised by one of their employees. Most definitely
not if the view is expressed in a meeting, with other people present. The
average boss will then believe they are being deliberately insulted, while
the person with autism has spoken out with every good intention. The
net result will be a conflict at work.'*

What are people with autism good at? What are their
qualities? We already know by now that they are detail-oriented,
careful, and have strong analytical skills. *'Many people with autism
are very creative,'* Annelies adds. *'In particular those with Asperger's*

have a lot of imagination. They regularly play computer games like "World of Warcraft". There are also people who make fantastically detailed drawings or sculptures. They see a city and then depict it in a drawing. The way they can focus on the details and copy them to perfection is an art in itself. They are very good at thinking in images and make beautiful works of art. Furthermore, people with autism relatively often have absolute pitch. So we can see that they may also be talented in the field of music. Another quality is that they stick to tasks for a very long time. Where someone else would have given up ten times already, they just keep going.'

'A characteristic of people with autism is their "bottom-up" approach to thinking and working,' Annelies writes in her dissertation. What does she mean by that? *'They start with the details. If they are writing a book, as you are now, they often start by researching all kinds of detailed information. They will, for example, draw up a long list of known people who have autism, or of the professions of these people. And they want to have such a list completed before they can continue. Whereas you probably first think up the outlines and develop an overview of what ought to be the global content of the book. Only then do you start looking for people with autism. They want to have all the details complete first – which takes much more time than when you start with the overview and fill in the relevant details after. There are also people with autism who can only work on the details and never get an overview. These people are great at keeping archives, for example, as they do not need to have that overview then. But there are also people with autism who are so smart that they not only have an image of the details, but also the overview. Those are people who can set up the archive. Both types of people have a "bottom-up" approach to thinking. The difference is that one group does get a total picture, and the other one does not.'*

If you were to apply all this to the matter of career options, what would be the most obvious professions for people with autism? We can think of the computer nerds ourselves. And we have already seen the line manager, the tax inspector, the software tester and the archive assistant. Annelies thinks it's a tricky question. She knows that she can never give an exhaustive account, and she does not want to exclude the professions she does not mention. In principle, there is no profession in which they really cannot practise. *'Someone with autism can, for example, very well be a manager, because he is so analytical that he knows exactly which people with what abilities need to be given which tasks.'* She also mentions the example of teaching posts. That is not the first thing to come to mind. But a number of people with autism with whom Annelies has worked are teachers and perform relatively well at it. *'Due to their detailed knowledge they know everything, and they are apparently good at passing it on. In addition, they are often very consistent and structured in class, which can be very beneficial to pupils.'*

Maybe it's better to specify the activities they are not good at. *'They should not be given general or global tasks, which leaves no room for getting into the details. This often makes them very restless. They prefer to do the things they can do very accurately. I also often advise against jobs in which tasks are continually changing. If there are changes, the employer must communicate them clearly and ensure that not too many changes are made at once. The tasks are preferably concrete and clear. Being able to work in an environment with few stimuli is important, too. They cannot be put in the middle of a big open-plan office, where everybody walks past them. That is too noisy a spot. Having to deal with unexpected social situations is also difficult for people with autism. These can occur during breaks and informal contacts with colleagues, and may make the person with autism feel very uneasy. It is difficult for them to meet implicit social expectations, such as speaking out to the boss on an important subject. For other people, it is a matter of course when this needs to happen. For them, it isn't.'*

People with autism tend to take language literally. Annelies talks about a discussion with a girl with autism in her practice. The discussion was about comforting. The girl said that only her mother could comfort her. Following which Annelies asked curiously: 'What is it your mother does, then?' The girl replied:

'She sells kitchens!' People with autism also have difficulty sensing when a conversation has ended. They often do not pick up on what is said between the lines, or body language. *'If you, for example, ask them to make some coffee, they will do so, but will not pour it out.'*

Can people with autism work full-time? *'Some can,'* Annelies says. Some? That means that most cannot. *'Yes, but I think that most people, also those without autism, should not work full-time.'* We laughingly concede that Annelies does have a point here. But regarding people with autism, Annelies thinks they can work full-time if everything is arranged perfectly and they feel totally at ease. *'But that is very difficult to achieve. The less suitable the workplace, the fewer hours they can work.'*

In her dissertation, Annelies writes that people with autism are slower at processing information. We can imagine that employers do find that a problem. *'Yes, except when you have tasks that need to be done very carefully,'* Annelies says. *'Checking tax returns, for example. There is no room for error there. It is better to have someone with autism do that. They may work somewhat slower but they do keep it up for longer and make relatively few mistakes. Other people get fed up at some point and then start making mistakes.'* The fact is that the tax inspectors are given targets they need to reach. They need to check X number of returns per month. Not too favourable for people with autism, then. *'If an employer expects a pace of work that makes it inevitable that employees will make mistakes, he had better not hire people with autism. Unless he offers them a lot of structure. When provided with a clear structure, some people with autism are able to work at a faster pace.'*

By now we have a clear picture of the requirements for work activities for people with autism. But where are they best placed? *'Research shows that they hold a technical job twice as often as other people do. This is linked to their focus on detail, and not so much to their lack of social graces. I quite like that, as it is the result of their strengths and does not have anything to do with their weaker side. In general, one could say that best use is made of their abilities in technical environments, but also in the creative sector and in administrative positions, thanks to their scrupulousness and focus on detail.'*

We understand that it is hard to give actual positions. Annelies mentions the archives assistant referred to above. *'In the first instance, this seems to be a suitable position for people with autism, but nowadays archives assistants also need to make contacts and call people up. And this suddenly poses problems. "Job carving" might form a solution. It involves dividing a position into those elements that are and those that are not suitable for a specific employee. By clustering tasks, three new positions are constructed out of three existing ones, one such position being custom-made for the autistic employee.'* This therefore requires action on the part of the employer. The organisation Annelies works for tries to involve employers in the region in the issue of autism. For example, it organised a conference on working with people with autism. A prize was awarded to the employer who managed to create the best working conditions for people with autism. When counselling people with autism, contact is often sought with the employer. The latter is then given advice for adapting tasks and workplaces, enabling the person with autism to work better. Fortunately, Annelies mainly encounters employers who are prepared to listen and actually do something with the advice they are given. *'We need to explain where profit can be made. We need to convince the employer that someone with autism is not an employee with an employment disability. In some areas, autism comes with very clear advantages. It can be an asset.'*

So people with autism can be successful? *'There is no reason whatsoever why they should not be. They can be successful precisely because they have very specific talents.'*

MINDFULNESS TRAINING FOR AUTISTICS

Annelies Spek provides a special mindfulness training for people with autism. Many people with autism have difficulty putting a stop to their thoughts. At night in bed, they can lie awake for hours worrying, for example, about something that happened at work. 'Normal' people let off steam by talking with other people about their problems. For people with autism, that is usually not the case. For them, social interaction is not the solution. Consequently, they lack a way of release. The participants in the training learn to use various meditation practices to re-focus their attention from their thoughts onto something concrete – for example, their breathing, allowing them to relax better. At work, too, they can use the meditation practice to avoid becoming overstimulated and overburdened. By briefly focusing their attention elsewhere, they make room in their heads for new information. In addition, by focusing attention on their body, they learn to notice signs such as fatigue or tension sooner, so they may take a break or seek relaxation by taking a short walk. Finally, there is a group who, after work, use meditation to clear their minds of work and make room for the family. The meditation training offers people with autism a tool to regulate their autism themselves.

The mindfulness training has been specially adapted for people with autism. In a training for 'normal' people you may, for example, be asked to imagine having a hole in your head through which you breathe, just like a dolphin. But you cannot ask that of people with autism. They don't respond to that. The training has been made more concrete and structured. In consultation with the participants the trainer establishes when they should practice during the day, for how long, where to sit, and whom to inform about it. That structure is very important.

5.

'AUTISM DOES WORK!'

Bram Barkhuysen is director of OBA Milestones BV organisatie voor Bedrijfs Architecten (Organisation for Company Architects). His company develops a digital portfolio for (young) adults with autism.

Both finding a job and keeping it is difficult for people with autism. They are not good at presenting themselves in a job interview or performance interview. A Dutch centre for autism has started a programme to make use of new technologies to improve opportunities for people with autism of finding a job. A digital portfolio forms a part of this programme. It involves creating a personal page on the internet, comparable to Hyves or Facebook, allowing people with autism to show who they are and what their competencies are. Their strong points are shown by means of texts, photographs and movies – but the less developed aspects are described as well. The portfolio is personal and very well protected.

Bram can absolutely be described as an enthusiastic entrepreneur. He is almost one with his product. We agree to meet him on a beautiful day at Motel Eindhoven (the Netherlands). We find a place on the terrace. The warm sun compels us to nod off a little, but Bram keeps us awake. He says right away that the portfolio will probably be augmented with a self-help manual, thanks to a European subsidy project (Leonardo). *'This will enable people to contact a coach who teaches them how to handle their autism and who focuses on the things people can actually do themselves. Because that is where we're heading. The unemployment agency is making drastic cutbacks. This means that people with autism have only limited access to a vocational expert, and that we are moving in the direction of digital governance. The portfolio can be uploaded at the internet environment of the unemployment agency…'* This is a little too quick for us. Let's start at the beginning.

Six OBA Milestones people work at the unemployment agency on a national client tracking system for young people who receive benefit under the Dutch Invalidity Insurance (Young Disabled Persons) Act; these are all young people with a disability. *'We are talking about 200,000 young people in the Netherlands,'* Bram says. *'The largest stream of people claiming benefits under this Act consists of young people with ADHD and ASD. People are already branded in their youth: you have PDD-NOS (Pervasive development disorder – not otherwise specified) and you have ADHD. Unless they are empowered by some manner of means, these youngsters will grow up to believe they can't do anything.'* And therefore they end up on benefits as well.

This is the present situation. The numbers are shocking and the point is immediately made clear. With the increasing number of young people claiming benefits under the Invalidity Insurance (Young Disabled Persons) Act, and the current cutbacks on personal assistance for people who have difficulty finding a job, it is wise to give these people tools with which they can start working independently, possibly with assistance from a distance, via the internet. But how exactly does this e-portfolio work?

'People with ASD create their own file on the internet, with personal information on education, internships, work experience, talents, handicaps, private circumstances… In fact, it contains everything that person wants to share. It can also contain photos and movies. That is the e-portfolio. When inviting people such as an employer, job or rehabilitation coach or a personnel officer to look at his or her portfolio, that person can make certain pages in the portfolio available or not. So the owner of the portfolio determines who gets to see what. He provides access rights. The structure of the portfolio is entirely

tuned to people with autism. The "My autism" button, for example, leads to information on circumstances that employers need to take into account if they want to hire the portfolio holder. "I prefer working alone in a room" or "I like to know long in advance exactly what I need to do" or "If this and that happens on the work floor, there is a risk that I will perform less well". But it may also be positive. "I am very good at…" You name it. So, on the one hand it is about the things they can do, the diplomas they have, the things they have already done. And on the other: what would an employer need to pay attention to, should this person come to work for them?'

The question is, of course, how smart someone needs to be to make the portfolio, but according to Bram you do not need to be very intelligent at all. The set-up is especially user-friendly. He even believes that many highly talented people with autism will not use it. They are much further ahead already and may not need it. On the other hand, it offers them, as well, the opportunity to present themselves. *'We are in consultation with, amongst others, the Dutch Ministry of Employment and Social Affairs to have it declared a public provision, the idea being that everyone, young and old, should have the opportunity to make an e-portfolio.'* We quite like this. It would place people with ASD in less of an exceptional position: have everybody who is looking for work or who wants to present themselves for whatever job create an e-portfolio. To Bram, this is of course a future aspiration.

'But for people with autism you need a portfolio that is custom-made. That is why we now provide a portfolio for young people who have to make the transition from school to work or advanced training, young people who, due to their behavioural handicap or psychiatric problems, experience a structural limitation in participating in education. There is also a digital portfolio for adults with ASD set up for the step from education to work, from rehabilitation to work or from one job to another.' Bram sees another big advantage in the e-portfolios. *'The e-portfolios put the people with ASD back in charge of their lives and eventually assist in more people finding work at less expense.'*

Can employers search in the e-portfolios for suitable people for their organisation? *'The people who have made the portfolio determine what happens with it. That is the basic point of departure.'* So not all and sundry can go snoop around? *'If someone with ASD applies for a position at a company, he may give the personnel officer of that company access rights to his portfolio or part of it. It may therefore also be the case that the applicant only does this after a few discussions have already taken place, and when there is a serious interest. The time is also determined by him.'*

Some scepticism is allowed here. Would such an e-portfolio not have a negative effect? When employers read about all the things they need to consider if hiring a person with autism, it may deter them from doing so. Aren't many employers hesitant about this? *'The portfolio doesn't emphasise people's handicaps but, on the contrary, focuses on their strong points. The idea is to make it into a type of talent bank. People with ASD who have an e-portfolio give the unemployment agency permission to include part of their portfolio in that talent bank. The unemployment agency then invites employers, say, Philips, to have a look in that talent bank. We already have the education system on our side, as well as the institutions and the rehabilitation agencies. The next step is to get the business sector involved.'* That doesn't seem like an easy task to us, but according to Bram, many companies are quite prepared to hire people with autism or another handicap. *'Let me give you an example. In our company, 60 per cent of people have something or other. I employ a very good programmer who was declared to be 50 per cent unfit for work due to back problems. I employ a school drop-out with ADHD. One of my best consultants has been declared 100 per cent unfit for work because he has an anxiety disorder. For all these people you have to consider their disabilities, but they perform excellently. There is almost no staff turnover. And,'* Bram says, pointing his finger, as a sign for us to pay extra attention now, *'the smallest man in the Netherlands works for my company. He is one metre and*

20 centimetres tall. He is married to the smallest woman in Europe, 80 centimetres tall. He has worked at OBA Milestones for three years and is an ambassador for young people with disabilities.'

This does put things into perspective. So Bram's company has things well organised, but that isn't a guarantee for all companies. *'You need to start with the success stories,'* Bram says. *'They are there. You have to show that it does work. "Autism does work!" In addition, more and more aids have become available. Consider a self-help manual linked to the e-portfolio, with which the employee with ASD can get online help during his work in case of problems. A type of coaching module. Or the iPod that has been developed by Dr Leo Kannerhuis[1] as a sort of TomTom navigation system for people with autism. It offers them advice on what to do when they end up in unexpected situations, like when they are en route and trains suddenly break down.'* We notice that many aids are focused on improving the coping skills of people with autism. Help people help themselves. That seems to be the key to success.

Does Bram foresee a rise in the use of IT-related support, such as the e-portfolio? *'The portfolio is a tool. It isn't an alternative for rehabilitation and suchlike. It needs to be provided in combination with proper coaching. If you are intelligent enough to complete the e-portfolio yourself, you will be all right. But you might need to call in assistance to do so — for example, from a rehabilitation agency. Thanks to the e-portfolio, less guidance is required. Many various institutions are involved in assisting people with autism, such as mental health institutions, rehabilitation agencies, the unemployment agency, you name it. The e-portfolio can link all these institutions with each other. And all the while, the people with autism keep control of the matter. It is a sustainable tool. Throughout your entire life you can add the things you have learned and the places you have worked. But it remains a tool, not a solution.'*

---

1   Visit www.leokannerhuis.nl and the Center for Autism in the Netherlands.

Bram is positive about the chances of people with ASD on the job market. *'Thanks to tools like the e-portfolio, these people are better able to show their abilities. Their job interviews are now entirely different. It also makes coaching people with autism easier and less expensive.'*

6.

CHICKEN À L'AUTISTE

Ted de Laat (68) is a pensioner but still works at the Andros Men's Clinic in Nijmegen, the Netherlands. Thea is his wife and has collaborated with him as a nurse at the Radboud University Nijmegen Medical Centre. Ted has Asperger's syndrome.

Ted de Laat stopped smoking over two years ago and now has another addiction: chewing gum. During the interview he calmly chews his gum. *'People with Asperger's cannot help being predisposed to addiction,'* he apologises. But it does not bother us. After 15 minutes his wife Thea joins us. In a totally relaxed and open atmosphere we talk in great detail with them about their experiences in the field of autism. About the gift Ted has that serves him well in his work, his long battle with the question of what was wrong with him, and the moment the penny finally dropped. We discuss what this means for their relationship, and how a man with Asperger's needs to adapt to be able to function successfully in society.

Ted is retired. He worked for 28 years at the Radboud Hospital in the urology ward, for the last ten years as physician assistant (PA). The PA works under the supervision of a specialist and carries out medical treatments a nurse is not allowed to do. Ted has benefited a lot in his work from his autism. He is a detailist, as he calls himself. He is better able to distinguish details on X-rays and ultrasounds than other people can – for example, when localising kidney stones. *'Sometimes you cannot see kidney stones in X-rays,'* he explains. *'You then have to make do with the ultrasound.'* But even then it is very difficult. And Ted excels at it. He is regularly called and asked if he can come by to have a look.

Ted still works two days a month in Arnhem and one day in Amsterdam at Andros Men's Clinic, a clinic that focuses entirely on providing healthcare to ageing men. The founder of that clinic, Professor Debruyne, also used to work at the Radboud University Nijmegen Medical Centre. He asked Ted to go with him to work in his clinic, although, according to Ted, it wasn't actually a question. *'He does not ask, he simply appoints you,'* Ted says with a touch of irony. But he likes it there. It is of course nice to be able to practise your profession a few days per month when you don't actually need to any more. Apart from pulverising kidney stones he performs tasks like prostate biopsies – taking a tissue sample from the prostate to check for cancer. *'I work in a very structured manner,'* Ted says. *'I need that to do the things I want to do.'*

As an example, Ted shows how he cooks for large parties, something he likes to do. First, he collects all the information from websites or magazines. He then draws up a menu and makes a perfect overview of all the ingredients, the amounts, what needs to go together, how long it has to cook for and in what order. It is a detailed step-by-step plan, which he only needs to follow to arrange the perfect dinner. *'You do need to explain how to read it,'* his wife Thea, who joined us at this point, says. *'Because I don't think it is easy.'* But then, Thea does not have Asperger's. Ted has by now gathered a nice supply of 'step-by-step plans'. *'When the billiard club comes for dinner, I only need to pick one out,'* he says. Once in a while he puts together a new dinner. *'Initially this is quite a lot of work, but it is a healthy investment because it really pays dividends,'* Ted says. It is an example of the way Ted works, i.e. in a structured and detailed manner. *'But there is something else,'* Ted adds. *'Ordinary people draw up a plan that they oversee and elaborate in detail. But I start from the ingredients and work my way up.'* So the other way around. Typical for people with autism. Later on in the conversation he says that he cannot cook any another way. He cannot open a cupboard and ask himself: Gee, what shall I make? He needs to prepare everything in advance, and the steps to be followed have to be written down. Nobody notices.

Back to his work. Why do they ask Ted and not somebody else? *'Can I say something?'* Thea asks. *'I have worked with him and also with others. He simply looks more thoroughly.'* Thea was a nurse at the department where Ted worked in the Radboud University Nijmegen Medical Centre. Ted adds: *'If you find an increased protein level in 100 people which could indicate prostate cancer, 20 of them will actually have cancer. So 80 people have had a biopsy taken for nothing. My score, though, is not 20 per cent but 40 per cent. So I only take 60 biopsies out of 100 for nothing.'* Based on the ultrasound images, Ted can therefore make a correct diagnosis twice as often as the average specialist. Ted shows an ultrasound image on his laptop. He points to something blurry which a trained expert could identify as a tumour. *'Everybody can learn to identify this,'* he says, *'but often it is not so clear. When I look at it, I get a certain feeling. Anybody else would then say it is a tumour, but I say that it isn't. I cannot explain exactly how that works with me. The reverse also happens – others going over certain spots too easily, and me wanting an additional image to have a better look at it. The Radboud University Nijmegen Medical Centre has spent millions on an MRI scanner. It should make it easier to determine whether someone has prostate cancer. It might result in biopsies no longer having to be taken at all. It has happened that, based on these MRI images, the doctors have informed patients that they have cancer. They subsequently came to me for the ultrasound. But I, based on the ultrasound images, saw that there was no tumour at all, and my view turned out to be correct. They scared the patients for nothing.'* That is why they still ask Ted to come and scrutinise ultrasound images. He is not a doctor or radiologist, but as far as judging ultrasound images for prostate cancer is concerned, he may be the best in the Netherlands.

Before becoming a PA, Ted was team leader for 18 years on the urology nursing ward. He managed a group of 23 nurses, although it is well-known that people with autism have trouble communicating. This does not apply to Ted. He simply is clear all the time. *'I said how things had to be done and that was it,'* he says. Thea knows all about that. *'I was the only one who occasionally disagreed with him and they thought that was wonderful,'* she says. *'He is fair but can also come across as very intimidating. But the people in his team all rallied around him. He is very honest.'* Ted: *'I could be rather authoritarian but I did know what I was talking about. I made sure I could explain and substantiate everything well, in great detail. So I was always right.'* Ted laughs. *'Thea sometimes says: "You always need to be right." And I retort: "But I am."'* Thea responds: *'You aren't always.'*

Looking back, Ted thinks that he chose to work in healthcare because of his autism. *'I took up nursing to learn about emotions. In an intense hospital ward you see a lot of emotion. In particular when someone is on their deathbed and the family is gathered round. There is, of course, sadness. If you see that often enough, someone with autism will eventually also recognise the feeling that is part of sadness in himself. At a certain point you feel these emotions. Not always, and only after some time.'* Ted realises that it is difficult to explain to people who do not have autism. Thea, who experiences it personally, makes an attempt. *'We may be very lyrical about emotions, but they are just physical reactions to stimuli. People with autism have a delay in that response. We immediately feel an emotion when we see something. People with autism may, on a rational level, assert that what they see is terrible, but the response only comes much later. Sometimes only after a day. Then they wonder what is wrong with them. They do not link it to the prior event. They may panic or become aggressive. If someone with autism knows that this may happen, he may be able to think of the event that caused this strange, upsetting feeling.'* This delayed processing of emotions can sometimes come in handy. Two years ago, Ted needed neck surgery. He knew he would not react emotionally to what he was told until the following day. The advantage was that he was able to listen closely to what the orthopaedist had to say. Because of their emotions, other people might forget half of what is said at such a time.

'His nursing job helped Ted to learn what behaviour goes with which emotions,' Thea explains. 'Consequently, he can now also explain this to himself. It is not the case that people with autism do not have feelings, but they often cannot interpret them. That is the problem.' In 2007 Ted and Thea visited the Bergen Belsen concentration camp in Germany, as Thea's father was involved in its liberation. In the camp they go their separate ways. Thea joins a group with a guide. Ted explores the camp by himself. 'There are horrible photographs there,' Thea says. 'They made me cry. I saw Ted standing in another room and he suddenly walked away. Something was wrong. He displayed what I call his "autistic walk". I went after him and saw him sitting outside on a bench. I asked him what was the matter. "Is it because you haven't had any coffee?" For there is no restaurant there. "No," he said. And: "Take all the time you need, do what you have to do and just let me sit here." Three days later, we were in the car and Ted said: "I have been trying for three days to tell you what happened to me there. Every time I want to start doing that, I have to cry." He started crying. Then he told me that he had been looking at all those horrible photographs of corpses dumped in pits, or starved camp inmates. And that he felt nothing. He was very upset that he didn't care. He then said that he walked on for a bit, to the next room, and then was suddenly seized with emotion. He said: "I stood there and became totally upset." Then I understood. It had to do with the different way in which people with autism process stimuli, with the delay. I explained that to him and it was a revelation for him. He now sometimes says: "I feel down, but it doesn't have anything to do with you. I do know where it comes from." He starts analysing it.'

Ted comes from a family of seven children and grew up near Den Bosch (the Netherlands), a small community where everybody knows each other. He had a few good friends whom he always played with. At home, he was a difficult boy. He had tantrums. While still at primary school, he was sent to see a psychiatrist on a number of occasions. He was also occasionally doped with sedatives. Every summer holiday he had to go to summer camp. *'The first year, I hated summer camp,'* Ted says. *'The other five years were all right. There was a lot of structure. After primary school I was sent to boarding school. That was very structured as well. I already sensed then that structure was good for me. I didn't like it, but this structure calmed me down. After completing the electronics training at secondary technical school, I had to do my military service. At that point in my life, too, everything was laid down for me. I followed NCO training and became a sergeant.'* During his time at secondary technical school, he regularly hung out in bars with friends, but didn't actually like what he was doing. *'We went out, for example, and sat in a pub. And I thought to myself: what am I doing here? Nothing at all happens. I once said that I thought we never discussed anything. But then they were taken aback.'* He then met Thea and a lot of things changed. They met on the birthday of a friend of Thea's. Thea thought Ted to be an unusual man, very introverted, which was evident from his body language. After only a week he told her: 'I will marry you.' Thea tried to explain that she thought it a little strange to say such a thing when they had only known each other for a week, but Ted persisted. Now they have been a couple for 40 years. According to Thea, a lot of women are attracted to men with autism. *'Because they have a neutral personality,'* she explains. *'They are not macho or predictable seducers. And they are real.'*

Ted has known since 2002 that he has Asperger's. *'He had already known for some time that something was wrong with him,'* Thea says. *'He felt he was different. Initially, he thought he had ADHD. I said: "Ted, you might have anything, but not ADHD, because ten horses cannot get you to budge." We decided to have him checked and find out. After a second visit to a psychiatrist in Den Bosch the conclusion was that I was to blame, as I was supposedly too dominant. I then told that man: "Now you listen. He wanted to come here. He has had his problem since birth and of course it influences our relationship, but our relationship is not the cause of his problem. I wash my hands of it. I am going." I have not gone along since. Ted was then prescribed Ritalin.'* Ted interrupts his wife: *'These pills made me very tense. They made my blood pressure go up.'* Thea: *'But they did make him feel less depressed. He was always depressed. He then stopped taking this medication and seeing that particular psychiatrist. Years later, in 2002, I read a piece in the paper about Martine Delfos's book on autism,* A Strange World.[1] *It was as if the world had been swept away from under my feet. I thought: this is it! I walked around with this thought for four weeks and then I told him. He sat there on his stool and I told him that I knew for sure what was going on with him. That he had Asperger's syndrome. "Now what?" was his reaction. I then went on to explore it further. If I get involved in something, I go for it 200 per cent. I also find it interesting. I also read about people with autism who make a very valuable contribution to the world, such as the English writer and essayist Daniel Tammet.'[2]*

Ted did in the end receive a diagnosis. But the road to it was dramatic. According to Ted and Thea, there are not enough support workers who approach people with autism as equal human beings. After a series of partly superfluous and time-consuming examinations, the Radboud University Nijmegen Medical Centre established that Ted had Asperger's. *'You are handed an enormous questionnaire,'* Ted says. *'You cannot even answer many of these questions because you don't know any more. For example, your Apgar score at birth. Or the question of whether you wet your bed as a child. All these lists are made for children.*

---

1   Delfos, M. (2205) *A Strange World.* Amsterdam: SWP Amsterdam. Her book describes in a clear and understandable way what autism is, paying extra attention to ASD and PDD-NOS.

2   Tammet, D. (2006) *Born on a Blue Day.* London: Hodder and Stoughton. In his book Tammet tells how he is able to mentally calculate complex sums of up to 100 decimal places, and learned Icelandic in one week. It is he who said: 'The line between remarkable talent and a remarkable handicap, surprisingly, seems extremely thin.' His book *Born on a Blue Day* was named Best Book For Young Adults in 2008 by the American Library Association. His various books have been published in 20 languages and he was elected as Fellow of the Royal Society of Arts in 2012.

Why do they not make a questionnaire for adults?' Being diagnosed brought enormous relief. It explains a lot. *'Also as regards how our relationship works,'* Ted says. *'Now, we can better explain emotions that bother me.'* *'I now know why certain things go the way they do,'* Thea adds. *'Living together with someone who cannot show how he feels or what he thinks can be quite difficult. Cohabiting with someone who has autism absorbs energy. You always need to pay attention to the way you communicate. If you speak a bit too hotly, or if you are excited with happiness, they will always say that you are picking a fight. With them, everything needs to be quiet, well organised and checked. And I am not quiet, well organised and checkable. So, it is difficult for both of us. His face does not show emotion either. And when I used to mention that, he would react with: "Yes, that is how my head is designed." Now I know why. I don't mention it any more. You also need to listen very carefully to what they say and not to how they say it, as that is often intimidating. If you comment on that, they react with surprise. He used to say things in an unpleasant manner first, and only later in a way that didn't bother me. That is still the case. I can understand that, but I cannot always manage not to mind. I sometimes have an off day as well. To the children he can sometimes be unintentionally blunt too. But they also understand that he can't really help himself. He doesn't always realise how he comes across.'*

Ted is very bad at remembering faces. Once when he was alone at home, the doorbell rang and he saw a completely strange woman who greeted him very cordially. He lets her in and had a cup of coffee with her. But even after she had gone, he couldn't recall who she was. Ted may walk past a good colleague on the street without recognising him. This often happens when he encounters people in places where he does not expect them. At parties too, he regularly has conversations with people he actually knows well, but does not recognise. Fortunately, Thea is close by to help him out. Ted doesn't really feel at ease at parties. He doesn't find it easy to chitchat with people. If Ted and Thea throw a dinner party for a large group of people, he likes to be in the kitchen. Then he is busy with his hobby and making himself useful, but does not need to engage in small talk. That is wasted on him. It quickly gets too crowded for him.

Ted does not look the people he talks to in the eye. He looks at the part of the face around the eyes. We don't notice that he's not actually looking at us. Ted has taught himself some little tricks to help him adapt socially. *'A necessity,'* he says. *'People with autism copy,'* adds Thea. *'They watch how we do things and communicate with one another, and then copy that. Ted now socialises but has copied it from me. Without knowing, I have always been his interpreter and coach, at work too. This was how he learned to show empathy toward his patients. I don't call them tricks either, I call them survival strategies.'*

'Just a practical matter,' Ted interrupts. *'I prepared a chicken dish with rice. Are you staying for dinner?'* Of course we don't say no.

One last question. Do Ted and Thea think that people with autism are given sufficient consideration by society? Thea thinks that people with autism are over-pampered. *'People are quick to tell someone with autism: "You don't have to do this, you aren't able to." And the bad thing is: if you say that to someone with autism, that's it, just you try to have that person "un-learn" it again… This applies to both children and adults. That way you block their development, and I think that is a real pity. I am convinced that if you put a child with autism in an environment with good examples, they can develop moral intelligence.'* Ted: *'In youth care, they put children with autism together with problem children, and even slightly criminal children. In so doing, they are providing bad examples to copy. As that's what autistic people do: they copy.'* But can someone who copies the behaviour of others still be himself? *'Yes, that is possible,'* Ted says. Is such a person not continually occupied with presenting himself differently from how he actually is? *'No, you make manners your own. After a certain point you are like that. You never become normal, but I don't feel abnormal either. Normal is the average of the sum total of deviations.'* So we all have deviations. *'Someone who is normal is boring,'* Thea says.

The meal is served. Chicken *à l'autiste*. It tastes great!

7.

'I CAN MAKE MY OWN CHOICES'

Robyn Steward (26) works as a specialist trainer to professionals and a mentor to people with autism. She is also an artist and musician.

On a Saturday morning in February we take the Northern line from King's Cross to Wandsworth, a borough in southwest London. After a short walk we arrive at the home of Robyn, an adult diagnosed with Asperger's syndrome. A few weeks ago we called her to ask her whether she would like to participate in our *AutiPower!* book project. 'I'd be happy to,' she answered. So here we are, at her front door and curious about what this woman might have to teach us. Because Robyn provides specialist training courses for professionals working with or supporting people who are on the autistic spectrum. She also mentors people on the autistic spectrum and their families. She has spoken internationally, at places such as University of California Los Angeles, and has appeared in several television and radio programmes. At the moment she is writing her first book about women on the autistic spectrum and safety.

A cheerful and enthusiastic lady lets us in. We sit down in a small room – a room with several paintings on the wall, painted by Robyn herself, as she tells us later. But before starting the interview she wants to show us a 'Squease vest'. Robyn leaves the room and returns a moment later with a sleeveless vest. She explains: *'It's for people with sensory difficulties* (possibly due to autism). *It comes with a hooded top, the vest zips into the top, making it discreet and mobile. And see, you can "squease" or inflate the vest with this hand pump. When it inflates, the vest pushes against my body. It gets bigger. That is pleasant to me, although it would not work for everyone. It's "deep pressure" and I feel more secure.'* On the website www.squeasewear.com we learn that the vest allows the wearer to regulate and apply soothing pressure in everyday situations that may have caused anxiety, stress or sensory overload, whether at home, at school or on the move. For people with sensory difficulties, who find dealing with change, busy environments or contact with other people highly stressful, applying pressure to the upper body may be calming, increase body awareness or improve attention and focus. Robyn promotes the vest on the website by saying: *'I find it hard to relax before I go to sleep. I use Squease before I go to bed, to relax and recalibrate my thoughts so that I worry less about the troubles in my mind.'*

Well, let's start the interview! Robyn found that typical jobs did not suit her, so she made herself a job, thereby becoming self-employed. We ask her to tell us about her work life. *'I teach teachers, social workers. I go and meet with them. I teach the theories around autism and get them to understand what it is like to be autistic, not just from my perspective, but using the experience of working with others to help them understand how different people are affected differently. I also teach them strategies and how to build strategies.'*

Of course, we are curious about how she does this. Robyn shows us one of her training workbooks. She created it herself. She says: *'One of the tasks I get people to do is around sensory issues. People work in pairs and I give them each a photograph and ask them to list the stimuli, things which stimulate your senses — for example, smell and touch.'* Robyn shows us a photograph of a street scene and asks us what we might smell — for example, food or the smell of the exhaust from the bus. And what differences particular clothing might make. Is it cold outside? Then she shows us a second picture of people in a train. Do we smell the people? Or the toilet? This helps social workers and support workers understand just how much sensory information there is in different environments and how one might become overloaded.

How often does Robyn train people? She laughs and says: *'Oh well, a lot. Don't know.'* Can we conclude that autism awareness is growing in the UK too? Robyn continues: *'In England we have the House of Commons and House of Lords. They decide about the law. Laws are part of Acts. An Act is just a group of laws. We have an Act for education, including education for people with special needs. We also have the Equality Act. This covers amongst other things gender, sexuality and disability. In 2009 the Autism Act became law, that's only about autism. The Act makes provisions about the needs of adults who have autism. It is the first ever disability-specific legislation to be passed in England.'* The Acts are very important, we hear from Robyn. Because of this Act every local authority has to provide training for social workers on autism.

Is the work exhausting for Robyn? *'Oh yes,'* she answers. *'Yesterday I was in Portsmouth. I did three workshops and a keynote. I was quite tired from talking. That's why I decided to use my songs about autism to teach people in the final keynote.'* We look at each other. Music? 'Can you show us?' Robyn jumps off the couch and grabs her guitar. Before she starts playing, she explains: *'I don't really like triangle sandwiches, particularly when I'm not wearing shoes or socks. Because your mouth is not a triangle, it's more of an oblong. Eating a triangle sandwich feels a bit strange. So I decided to make my own shape, the "hexgazmela." It's a made-up word. I wrote a song about it. It highlights difficulties people with autism can have with particular things like triangle sandwiches.'* Then Robyn starts to sing. We are surprised. That's a good way to explain autism! Touched by our enthusiasm, Robyn plays and sings a few more songs. One is about her thoughts of Facebook. She explains beforehand: *'On Facebook you can unfriend a person. A lot of people on the autistic spectrum can become upset about this. They may ask themselves: someone is not my friend any more? But a Facebook friend is not the same as real friend. A real friend is someone who cares about you. They don't unfriend you. Friendship is about respect. Friends on Facebook are different. And those messages that you get on Facebook… For example: "If you don't re-post it, you will die." You won't die if you don't re-post them. But people on the autistic spectrum sometimes think they* will *die! People take it literally. So I wrote this song about Facebook.'* Robyn feels *'Facebook is really silly.'* After her Facebook song it's clear: Robyn makes a point with this way of teaching. What a creative person she is! *'It's a way to communicate with people,'* she says. *'And people remember songs.'*

'I have always been creative. As a kid,' she continues, *'I wrote stories. Lots of stories about outer space. Stuff I had seen on television. I didn't like* Star Trek, *but sometimes I watched it. So I wrote my own story, for example about the year 1999. I was eight at that time. I also wrote poems. I was quite good at poetry. But I was not really known for my creativity at high school. I also paint with acrylics using my fingers. I have hundreds of paintings.'* Talking about her childhood, did Robyn feel different from other children? *'Yes,'* she answers. *'For example, I was gullible and this could be something people were able to use to bully me.'* Robyn was diagnosed when she was a little girl. Her mum had already known, when Robyn was only a few months old, that she was autistic. *'I didn't cuddle up to her. And when I was older, I didn't point at things. Didn't make eye contact or pay attention. So she started to play a guitar and sing to me, she enjoyed it and I was interested. That was the bridge, the connection between my mum and me. Music is also a connection to other people. Other people like music as well. So I made connections with other people, that didn't make me feel uncomfortable.'* When she was eight, her teacher referred her to CAMHS (Children and Adolescent Mental Healthcare Service). This was because Robyn did not settle well into a new class, while other children with severe behavioural problems did. So her teacher was concerned. *'The diagnosis took a while. Now we are more experienced in dealing with autism, especially in diagnosing girls.'*

Life was not uncomfortable for Robyn until the age of eleven. *'I was bullied somewhat, but compared to the last year of primary school and then high school, it was easy. In primary school the teachers liked me. I had friends. Friends like to come over to someone's house. I didn't really have such friends in high school. It was a lonesome period. My best friend was the IT teacher. I have a picture!'* Robyn is proud to show us a picture of this man. We look at it in surprise. He seems to be a nice and handsome guy. *'See, I knew you would react like that,'* Robyn laughs. *'He's handsome to other people, but to me, he is just my former teacher. He was kind of a friend. He would just let me sit in the IT room. I followed him everywhere around school, I was like his little shadow. Looking back, I am so grateful that he never told me to go away. We had a few arguments. But in general we got on and he was prepared to listen. I had a lot to say. That made the difference. Rather than tell me to stop asking questions, he just limited me to three a day. This really helped my self-esteem. Because at the time I was struggling in most of my classes, so rather than fail at social interaction, I just had some rules to work with. People on the autistic spectrum are often good with rules.'*

At this point in her life, Robyn already knew that she had Asperger's. What did the diagnosis change for her? *'By then I knew that I was not mad, insane or crazy. I knew that there were other people like me, for example, other people with Asperger's. I felt relieved. I found out about Asperger's when I was twelve, in my first year at high school. It was an awful year. They called me names. They locked me up in toilets. My big fear was toilets. The kids picked up on my anxiety. I don't like toilets. Even in my home, I don't lock the bathroom. You know when the door is closed that there is someone in there. I am an adult now, with my own home, and therefore I can control my rules, including the toilet. So, regarding my diagnosis, I asked my mother why I was different. Then she told me I had Asperger's. I knew I had something because I had seen a psychiatrist. I have a lot of disabilities.'* Robyn was born with ten disabilities, including cerebral palsy (a condition that affects muscle control and movement), dyslexia (learning difficulty, making reading and spelling difficult) and dyspraxia (difficulties with sequencing tasks, memory and coordination). *'I also have prosaprognosia* (face blindness). *I don't recognise faces, including my own. That's one reason why I wear a purple hat. So I can recognise myself in pictures. In the past I had blue hair, but that is expensive. You can wear a hat for a whole year!'* We look at each other. Robyn has had a lot of bad luck. How did she cope? Robyn laughs: *'I don't know what I miss. I get on with it. That's all you can do. I think about what I can do, not about what I can't. I only realise that I am disabled when I am with, or see, somebody else. When I am on my own or with my parents, I don't notice it because it has always been like this.'*

We admire how Robyn goes on with her life. She is so creative, positive and full of ideas. In 2013 her first book about women on the autistic spectrum and safety will be published by Jessica Kingsley Publishers.[1] She is very excited about her book. *'It's about safety. It now comes to 104,045 words! That's like 400 pages. Do I like writing a book? It makes me anxious. I have an editor at Jessica Kingsley. She helps me a lot, they really understand me.'* Robyn must be proud about having a book published. And she is! *'I can't wait until I can hold it in my hands. Now, it's just an abstract concept. Then, I will see that it's real. Now, it's all in my head, not yet a book.'* We agree. It's the most beautiful moment when you actually 'smell' and 'feel' your book. *'And I want to taste it!'* Robyn says enthusiastically.

Robyn is very productive. She is self-employed, provides training courses and has written a book. But we hear from other people with Asperger's that it is very hard to get a job in the UK. *'It's terrible,'* Robyn says. *'Only 15 per cent have a paid job.'* It sounds like a waste of talent. What does Robyn think of this situation? *'The problem is, many employers are scared. What does it mean to have an autistic employee? What adjustments do you have to make? Does it cost money? And a lot of people with autism who do work are bullied. This could be solved with some training/coaching for the non-autistic employers, as well as the person on the spectrum. For example, my college class thinks I'm annoying because I know a lot of things due to the way my memory works. When a question is asked, I answer it because I know the answer. But I have learned to try to wait for others. This is hard for me. But being on the spectrum has its uses. I can be useful. There were three girls in my class who wanted to write*

---

1   Steward, R. (2013) *The Independent Woman's Handbook for Super Safe, Living on the Autistic Spectrum.* London: Jessica Kingsley Publishers.

books. I know a little about it. I explained about the royalties, advance and contract, etc.'

So, we can conclude that it's hard for people on the autistic spectrum to get a paid job. And that this is a pity, because people on the spectrum can have useful skills. What needs to change? Robyn thinks for a moment and says: *'Neurotypical people have to be more open to us. We need to help each other. Everybody has their own skills. When we talk about autism, we look at deficits, we don't look at abilities. When we talk about neurotypicals, we always talk about abilities, not deficits. Neurotypical is the standard. So currently having autism is a disability, being neurotypical is not. But you can argue both ways. Autism is a disability, to some extent, only because the majority of the world is not autistic. Of course, many people who are autistic also have a learning disability. And clearly this can make life very challenging. Sensory issues are also an issue. But a lot of the social difficulties would be less noticeable if the majority was not neurotypical.'* Robyn thinks that it's important to have a balance of people – some autistic people, and some neurotypical people.

How does Robyn see her future? *'I am not sure,'* she answers. *'I worry a lot. Even if my calendar is filled with training work, there needs to be other things as well. I have to expand my business. I want to sell my paintings more often and would like to release an album.'* And this happens! A few months after our interview with Robyn, she tells us that she has worked with Mark Ty-Wharton (see Chapter 19) on an album. Their first single, *@ space Cadet@*, was released on World Autism Awareness Day 2013. It's available on ITunes and all good digital music outlets. When Robyn and Mark collaborate on music projects together, they call themselves ARRAY.

So Robyn has many possibilities. *'But people must see them. See my paintings and buy them. I don't know what is going to happen in the future, which makes me anxious. I didn't plan to do anything with autism. I planned to go to university and become an IT technician. But not so many people with autism have jobs. So I took the opportunity to be self-employed and teach people about autism.'*

Even though Robyn feels a bit unsure about the future, does she think she is successful? *'Yes, I feel successful, but not in the usual sense of the word. I do a lot of different things. I have friends and a job. But I still don't earn a lot of money. It depends on the definition of success.'* Maybe we should ask: 'Are you happy?' *'Well, sometimes I feel unhappy. But that is an autism thing. But I am lucky with the job I have now. I like it and it allows me to make my own choices. And that is very important to me.'*

FROM ROBYN'S WEBSITE, WWW.ROBYNSTEWARD.COM

You may have seen the film *Rain Man*. Raymond in the film was based on a real-life man named Kim Peek. He had Kanner Autism and savant syndrome. His amazing abilities with numbers came from savant syndrome, as opposed to autism, and therefore are not shared by everyone with autism. Kanner Autism is known as low-functioning autism. The other end of the spectrum is Asperger's syndrome, sometimes referred to as high-functioning autism. Notable people with Asperger's are Gary Numan and Ladyhawke. After careful research of behavioural traits, many famous historical figures – such as Einstein and Newton – are thought to have had Asperger's. However, it is important to understand that, while someone may be labelled as high-functioning or as having a mild form of autism, autism still affects them. Everyone has different needs and it is important to find out a person's needs.

There can be some very positive aspects to having autism, such as being a hard worker, dedicated, able to focus, honest and having a very good memory and close attention to detail. Everyone's skills are different, though. Not everyone will go on to have a world-famous career, but this does not mean they do not make an important contribution in life. Equally, not every autistic will live in a care home or remain single. Everyone with autism is different.

8.

THE INTERESTING EXPERIMENT

Frank van Tiel (45) lives alone, apart from his partner. Frank works as software engineer at a small company. After seeing a documentary on autism ten years ago, he discovered that he was autistic. Frank dedicates himself to people with autism. He is among others member of the board of PAS [People on the Autistic Spectrum] Netherlands, the Dutch association of normal to highly gifted adult persons with a disorder in the autism spectrum. (See box on p.80.)

When we visit Frank van Tiel, it becomes clear he is a true nature-lover. There are pictures on the wall of a nest of blackbirds growing up. A dead beetle, little skulls and stones are placed on top of the TV. Frank finds all this in his town garden, which is also a veritable oasis for house sparrows. He shows us a picture he made of the tree in his garden. 'It houses 82 sparrows,' he says, stating the exact number. We look at him in astonishment. We are no less astonished when we come to listen to his story. He is glad to know finally that he has ASD. *'I might well have ended up badly otherwise.'*

'I have actually always found myself in the right place by accident,' Frank says. He tells us about the road that led him to his current job. *'I started studying information technology, but it might just as well have been chemistry. The fact is that I had a nine for chemistry on my school leaving report. But on the open day of the laboratory school I noticed that it was absolute chaos there. I could not find anything. Later, I went to the open day of the technical college for*

information technology. Everything was structured there. That is the reason why I chose information technology.' After completing his studies Frank was unable to find a job. He was unemployed for a year and a half. He finds it hard to market himself. *'I cannot present myself better than I am without coming across as unreliable.'* Then, an opportunity turned up: Frank participated in a pilot project for retraining foreigners for the automation field. *'They wanted to obtain good results for that pilot and were looking for people who would be sure to do a good job. As I am officially a foreigner – my father was born in Curacao – this project fitted me to a tee. So I set to work on it. After completion of this assignment, they linked me to the job vacancy section and arranged, among others, an interview at Infra Design. I was given a few IQ tests. One of these was called "Letter Series", as written in beautiful letters above the test. I was the only candidate who, with the vision of an autist (although I didn't yet know I was one at the time), saw that the spelling was not right. There were three t's instead of two. I was frank enough to point this out to them. This almost certainly played a role in the decision to hire me.'*

Frank started working at Infra Design well over 16 years ago. The company was, however, later taken over by Ordina. The R&D department Frank worked in did not fit into the new company's structure, and it was therefore decided to have the department continue as an independent company. *'They proposed that we started up one-man businesses. So they wanted me to switch to being a self-employed person as well. I thought that was too much of a hassle. You have to take far too many things into consideration. Look at how I deal with my tax papers. I do nothing with the tax-deductible items. I fill out everything in the standard format. I let them handle it. All these other things are completely outside my range of competence.'*

Frank is now employed by a small company. He feels at ease there. This does not mean to say that both Frank and the other people in the company did not encounter problems with his 'being different'. *'My technical brilliance made up for a lot. But I kept myself to myself a lot and I also had my own ideas. I had trouble accepting the ideas of other people. My communication skills were not strong. Fortunately, the department had no direct customer contacts.'*

How many hours does Frank work a week? *'Forty,'* he says. But isn't that a bit too much for someone with autism? *'Yes, in truth it is. In order to make a few hours less per week, I sometimes give up a holiday. Even then, I sometimes get into trouble. Doing a lot of programming is no problem. But there are times that I need to visit people all over the country. That takes up a lot of energy.'* So his work does demand quite a bit of his energy. Frank still is quite active outside of it, however. He is a committee member at PAS Netherlands, the Dutch association for gifted people with autism, and takes care of member administration, arranges for the manning of information stands, coordinates the hiking club and compiles the newsletter, together with his girlfriend, who is also autistic. He does not have a social life outside of these activities. He does not feel the need for it. At weekends, Frank takes a rest or spends time in the countryside with his girlfriend.

For a long time, Frank did not know that he had ASD. He hardly gave a thought to himself. He nevertheless noticed at some point that he was thoroughly overstepping his boundaries. Slowly, he realised that something was the matter with him. *'Ten years ago, I happened to see a documentary on TV about a man with Asperger's syndrome. I had a checklist in my head of the things that were wrong with me. With each sentence that this man said, I could tick off an item on my list. I could not interact with people either. I had never yet had contact with a woman.'* Frank surfed the internet to find out more about Asperger's. But the information he found was confusing. Frank lacks some of the characteristics of Asperger's syndrome. *'But at the time, you needed to have them to actually be diagnosed with Asperger's. Fortunately, I also came across an article in which all this was put in perspective. It had become clear that I really do have ASD. This doesn't necessarily have to be Asperger's. A name – what does that say, after all? This classification of syndromes within an autism spectrum disorder can be totally disregarded, or so I have discovered by now. It simply does not make any sense.'*

Some time later Frank met an assistant social psychologist who was employed at a mental health institution, where he was the only member of staff working with adults with autism. *'In a sense, we have trained each other. At one point, my rate of development was a lot faster. I then continued by myself. I did have a diagnostic conversation with this man. He concluded that I did have a condition on the autism spectrum. But as this was the conclusion of an assistant social psychologist and not a psychiatrist, it doesn't count as an official diagnosis. For me, this is irrelevant. I know it to be true. That's what matters. The only time I brought up the conclusion of this assistant worker was during the transfer from Infra Design to Ordina. I had to work in an open-plan office. I could not do this and did not want to. As a requirement under the Dutch Occupational Health and Safety Act, I said I wanted an office of my own. I got no response. That is why I asked the social-psychologist worker to write Ordina a letter. And, sure enough, I was the only non-manager to get an office of my own.'* Frank laughs. *'It was a small glass room, but with a door that could be shut. All those telephone conversations, the talking among people, I cannot stand that.'* Frank tells an anecdote about how sharp his hearing is. *'At Infra Design, my workplace was at one end of a long hallway, the toilets were at the other end. At some point, I was coming back from the toilet and a colleague said that I had had a phone call. I said: "Yes, I know." He looked at me in astonishment. I explained to him that I could recognise the sound of my own telephone from the toilet.'*

The problems Frank experiences as a result of his autism include some sensory issues. He has extremely good hearing. Sounds can be extremely loud to him. Especially if they are soft. This also goes for the chirping of the birds in his garden. *'I enjoy their presence… But I am very happy with the earplugs I wear almost constantly.'* Another aspect of his autism is that he has no idea what friendship is. *'The entire aspect of interhuman emotions is totally beyond me. I have been able to redefine friendship as something that does not necessarily have to include feeling. But I don't know what love, hate, jealousy and suchlike are. My "wiring" is totally different from that of people who don't have autism. It does give me a better eye for detail than most people.'* Can Frank be dubbed insensitive? *'No, as I do have certain sensitivities. Nature, for example, is my passion. It is definitely not the case that I am insensitive. If someone talks to me about an accident, I don't feel anything. But if I am involved, it is an entirely different matter.'* Frank does have a girlfriend. What does their relationship look like? *'Our relationship is not based on love. We are friends. The main reason things go well between us, is that we do not have expectations of each other. There is no dependence. We can both be ourselves. We have made a conscious choice not to live together. It is very hard to adapt to the other person. At most, we go on a one-week holiday together. We went to Ireland for a fortnight once. Halfway through the second week things started to get difficult. We managed to get through it. We were lucky that we had to rely on each other. We were staying at a lake with a few remnants of a village. We arrived there on a stormy night. Because we had not closed the gate properly, we discovered the next morning that the garden was full of sheep. We left it like that for the rest of the week. We went on wonderful walks and didn't see a living soul. Because we didn't experience any outside pressure, we could survive the inside pressure.'*

After seeing the TV documentary as described above, it seemed Frank had discovered how to flip his switch. It was not easy. He fell into a crisis. *'I went through the development that other people with autism go through over a number of years, in a few months. It is intense. You have to redefine yourself. I handled that in a very autistic manner. I used to think in absolutes. Things are as they are. I had a strong opinion about everything. I turned all those absolute absolutes into absolute relatives in a few months' time. Everything is relative. The gravity here is currently 9.81 metres per square second. I assume that this is correct. If it changes, well, then, I'll take it from there. By not thinking in absolutes any more, I am now better at handling other people's opinions. If someone is convinced of the truth, he is welcome to think so. I let it rest. That is an important strategy. I did have to accept, however, that I have to walk around with earplugs all day long at home. I cannot bear the slightest noise from the neighbours. I have an airco near my bed, as well as in the living room. I regularly switch it on at night, as an antidote. I then have a regular sound that drowns out the other noise.'*

What did Frank's childhood look like? He must have noticed being 'different'. *'I do not have many memories of that time. I was not interested in myself. I thought of myself as a loser. I went through life. That was it. I actually did not experience puberty. Going to school, studying, looking for a job, buying a house and looking for a partner. It was expected, nothing more. It was pure coincidence that I managed to do most of these things. Actually, I didn't do anything about it myself. And this acute sense of hearing, I thought everybody suffered from it. The only thing was that other people handled it differently. Those hard sounds were part of it.'* Frank used to find himself uninteresting but now he dares to say out loud that he is actually a worthwhile person. *'I consider myself to be an interesting experiment. What I went through in those few months after the autism diagnosis, is almost impossible. I do not recommend it to others. That length of time is much too short to go through such a development. I almost went under. I took sleeping pills and anti-psychotics. But I still did not sleep. I was awake for eleven nights in a row. In that period I was even on the brink of jumping off a bridge. That was not just an idea. The plan was ready.'* But suppose Frank had never found out that he was autistic, how would he see life now? *'Then I would actually have jumped off that bridge and be dead now,'* he answers immediately. *'Not because I was bonkers. No. I wouldn't be able to go on any more. If I hadn't seen that documentary, I would have spiralled further downwards into being a loser. I knew that I was. But I didn't look at it properly. I was not interesting. That documentary forced me to have a good look at myself. The documentary saved my life.'*

Frank's life could have gone in yet another direction. Autism is now being discovered at an increasingly early age. Frank is glad that this did not happen in his case. *'I know someone the same age as me. He also has the same abilities. This man has known that he has autism for most of his life. Consequently, he has been pampered by everybody his entire life. "Oh, but he can't do any better," they said about him. Now, he lives in a supervised home and works in a sheltered workshop. I, however, have learned to develop myself and be independent.'*

But where is the tipping point? What moment in life is appropriate for discovering that you are autistic? Frank thinks this is a difficult question. *'You cannot expect parents to continue treating their child normally and force it to develop normally when they hear that the child has a condition on the autism spectrum. I hardly know any young diagnosed person who does not receive benefit under the Dutch Disablement Assistance (Young Persons) Act. A number of them don't need it. But well, they got into it by chance. They don't need to do anything any more. Parents and care professionals should pay less attention to such a child. Pamper them less. People with autism are people. They are not autistics with a touch of humanity. Of course, at a certain point you are asking too much of such a person with this kind of strategy. Not every autistic person can indicate clearly when things are too much. But if you give in to them every time they protest about doing something, they never learn to stand on their own feet.'*

'I don't call myself successful,' Frank answers when we ask him whether he thinks he is. *'I am a sequence of coincidences.'* We look at each other in astonishment. Frank redefined himself within three months. That cannot be a coincidence? *'Okay, I actually did that myself. This is due to my highly developed intelligence. Once I think about myself, it's at a level that most people don't reach. I notice so often that I have a very broad and quick way of thinking, and that I can envisage many scenarios simultaneously. At the beginning of that period of rapid development I was doing that continuously. Now, I pick the right strategies.'* So…a successful autistic person after all? Frank is not convinced. *'If so, you need to define what part of me is the "autistic". Every person with autism is different. You should not compare me as I am now to a 20-year-old with autism. At the time, I stood completely outside society. I couldn't imagine joining a club. Certainly not if there were other people involved. Now I have started a hiking club within PAS Netherlands. Instead of joining something, I arrange it myself. For sure, I have scored victories over*

myself.' Frank mentions another example. During the world football championship, Frank came home after a bike ride. Half the neighbourhood was out on the streets. Everybody was busy hanging up flags. Neighbours were talking to each other. Frank did not run away but stayed and mingled. He had developed the necessary social skills to handle such a situation. He does not enjoy it, but nevertheless he does it. *'I have more contact with people from the neighbourhood now, which does have its advantages. If something technical needs to be done in the house, the neighbour opposite is ready to help me. If the neighbours have problems with their PC, they ask me for help. Not that I look forward to doing it, but I still do it because I think it is part of the deal.'*

We broach the autism and work subject with Frank. Can people with autism be useful for employers? Frank makes a comparison. *'Replace the word "autism" with "blond hair". How interesting is that? It isn't. Dealing with autism on the workfloor calls for rather a simple adaptation. Look at me in my own little office. When a colleague comes to me with an assignment, this too calls for just a small adaptation. I explain to this colleague that he has to go to my boss with his request. My boss then determines where my priorities lie and how much time I need to spend on assignments. I cannot create that structure myself. I am a typical scatterbrain. These are the adaptations that are necessary for me as a person with autism. So, minor ones. People with blond hair probably need other adaptations. It doesn't matter who you are. Of course, there are autistics who need more than a few minor adaptations. They can only function in a supervised workplace. But that also applies, for example, to people with Down's syndrome functioning at a higher level. You always have to consult with the person in question as to whether he could participate in the regular work process if some small adaptations were made. The fact that he is autistic does not matter. We often, wrongly, emphasise the advantages of autism, or the characteristics thereof. Both lists are useless. They are lists of characteristics, while the human being is the central point.'*

Frank does not call himself successful. Yes, at work things are going well, but as a human being? *'That is the bottleneck. Things could still be so much better. I regard myself as an average person. Do I still want to improve myself? I think I have reached my maximum.'* A nice experiment. That is Frank. But also a human being, like all of us.

PAS [People on the Autistic Spectrum] Netherlands is the independent interest group for (and run by) gifted adults with ASD. PAS Netherlands is involved in looking after the interests of people, stimulating expertise, providing education and information, organising contacts with other people with autism through contact days, discussion groups and suchlike, and organising activities. PAS has its own hiking club. PAS tries to let the voice of adults with ASD be heard through participation.

9.

'WE NEED MORE SUPPORT'

Maxine Aston is a Relate-trained couples counsellor in the UK, specialising in couples, families and individuals affected by Asperger's syndrome.

Maxine Aston is one of the very few counsellors specialising in working with couples, families and individuals affected by Asperger's syndrome. The majority of her work consists of helping couples in which one has Asperger's syndrome, to make their relationship work. On her website we read that, apart from counselling, Maxine gives lectures and workshops and has four books and a series of articles published. Her latest book is entitled *What Men With Asperger's Syndrome Want to Know About Women, Dating and Relationships.*[1] She sounds like someone who really knows what it is to have Asperger's syndrome and what challenges it creates. So we met her to see what she could teach us.

Maxine works with people with Asperger's and was once married to a man with Asperger's syndrome. So one of our obvious questions is whether this marriage was the cause for her choice of profession. But it wasn't. Maxine tells us: *'My ex-husband was diagnosed after our divorce. I don't believe it was because of the complications of Asperger's that our marriage ended.'*

'One of the things I always say to clients is, Asperger's syndrome does not change personality. It is not going to make somebody nice, nasty, good or bad. They are who they are. It only affects a small part

---

1   Aston, M. (2012) *What Men With Asperger's Syndrome Want to Know About Women, Dating and Relationships.* London: Jessica Kingsley Publishers.

of the brain. It is very similar to dyslexia, but rather than affecting reading, writing and spelling, it's going to affect communication, social interaction, empathetic thoughts and mindreading. These are all skills that are pretty important to help relationships run smoothly.'

Maxine tells us that she started her education late in life. But once she got going she made up for lost time: she started with a degree in psychology, then took a master's degree in health psychology. At the same time Maxine was training as a therapist and couples counsellor, and that was where her mission started. *'I remember that, while pursuing my degree, we watched a video about a couple with Asperger's syndrome. It reminded me of some of my clients, the kind that had been going through the mill for maybe 20 years trying to figure out what was going on. I raised it with one couple. The gentleman went on to be actually diagnosed and it completely changed their relationship. They had been a foot away from a divorce court, and understanding Asperger's resulted in their understanding each other and learning to communicate. That was it. That was the beginning of my mission.'*

'Mission' is not too strong a word. Maxine feels very strongly about her work for people struggling with the Asperger's syndrome and about the way healthcare professionals and society are treating them. *'There should be a better understanding and acceptance and less of a stigma attached to the term Asperger's syndrome. People, even GPs, have a stereotype of severe autism. Asperger's syndrome should be seen as just a difference. If people could see that and could see the qualities that can come with Asperger's syndrome, there wouldn't be so many people with Asperger's who are unemployed. To achieve a better understanding of Asperger's, we need more support from the government, therapists, teachers, universities, everyone. Asperger's syndrome and the relevance of understanding it should be in the training curriculum for all therapists and counsellors. At present, many healthcare professionals think that Asperger's syndrome is an excuse. It is not! It is a reality. Asperger's has a major impact on the life of the person affected by it. Most people with Asperger's syndrome will be struggling and at some time end up sitting in front of a therapist. And that therapist can either make things better, or completely wipe them out by ignoring them.'*

Unfortunately, Maxine has come across many examples of therapists not knowing how to coach someone with Asperger's syndrome: *'I remember hearing about a couple who went to a therapist who actually advertised that they worked with Asperger's, and they were asked "How long has he had this disease?" The couple knew enough to walk out. I have had clients who have been given communication exercises to do, such as go home and sit down for five minutes and talk about emotions with their partner. Naturally the Asperger's syndrome partner can't do it, this upsets the non-AS partner, and the couple end up arguing and possibly separating because of an uneducated therapist.'*

It is obvious that Maxine is very passionate about her work. We want to know more about how it actually works. Why do people come to her? Do they already know that they have Asperger syndrome? How does counselling start? We have so many questions we decide to just let Maxine explain how it goes. *'When I started as a counsellor, Asperger's wasn't quite so well known. Nowadays, clients have often read an article, picked up a book or seen something on television. In the majority of cases they have a child that is diagnosed with Asperger's. Of course, they start with getting help for the child – and suddenly the light goes on. Other clients come to me because I do assessments, but that is often only a starting point. The clients that I see are often in good jobs, they are married or with partners, they have children. It is often the partner who is actually aware that something is not quite as it should be. They can't figure out why they are not communicating, why every time they try and talk, it breaks down. And then we start working. There is no actual therapy written for people with Asperger's, so I don't follow a specific method. There is no rule book. The work I do is very structured, very honest. It is not about expecting them to gain insight and suddenly expect them to work it out for themselves. It really is saying what you mean and meaning what you say. The majority of my clients embrace that, because this is all they are looking for, they want somebody to be honest with them.'*

Saying what you mean and meaning what you say. That must be the key for couples dealing with Asperger's. Is that the first advice Maxine would give couples? *'Probably. And also: be realistic. But for all couples I have three rules for communication. Rule 1: No physical abuse. No threat of physical abuse. No intimidation. Rule 2: No verbal abuse. And that includes sarcasm, shouting, raising your voice, being intimidating. Rule 3: No bringing up the past.'* The first two rules seem obvious, and Maxine goes on to explain the third: *'We have no defence against the past. You can't change it! I tell couples, there is life before you realised about Asperger's, and there is life after. You have to wipe the slate clean so it is a new relationship and you get to know each other all over again. You almost go back to the courting stage.'*

This is, of course, the moment where we can ask one of the questions we really wanted to ask in this interview. Would Maxine be able to provide us with an example of a couple for whom counselling was successful? Maxine laughs and says: *'Yes, of course, I have a wonderful story. I once worked with a couple who must have been somewhere in their sixties. The wife explained that when she tried to discuss emotions with her husband, he would retreat. He was very passive, needed his autonomy, and needed his own time. His wife couldn't understand why, after a long day at work, he walked in and would not talk to her. She would become more demanding, more emotional, more upset. And the more she became upset, the more he distanced himself because he didn't know what to do. All he wanted to do was to make her happy, but he didn't know how. The husband didn't know he had Asperger's. It was his wife who read an article in* The Mail *and went looking for my website. At the time they came to see me, she was very upset and said she couldn't carry on and was going to end the marriage, which would have been devastating for the entire family. The fact that he suffered from Asperger's syndrome was discovered and in time they figured out what they could do together, even if it wasn't doing the same thing. One was interested in photography and the other was into walking, and they learned a way to combine the two. They built up their life again together and now they are absolutely rock-solid.'*

The way Maxine tells us this story brings tears to our eyes. This must be such gratifying work to do. Maxine confirms this: *'Yes it is rewarding, but not always.'* She tells us something we have suspected before, but which is sad to actually hear a specialist confirm: *'I am increasingly finding that there is a certain vulnerability to people with Asperger's syndrome. Most of the men I see are very passive. One of the ways they feel they can make their partner happy is by buying things for her. What is happening a lot is that they are unfortunately falling into the wrong hands. In my opinion they are being abused, being controlled.'*

Learning more about the challenges people with Asperger's syndrome face in their relationships and in daily life, we wonder what can be done. Is there any way that people with Asperger's syndrome can change to make their life happier? To our relief Maxine replies that yes, people with Asperger's can actually change. But it is not going to be easy! *'One of the things about people with Asperger's syndrome is that if they commit to a plan they will do their absolute best to achieve it,'* Maxine says. *'However they will only put effort into something they feel will help towards what they want to achieve. If this is the case and the couple are prepared to bond, change can be achieved. They can learn to make time to communicate, but it has to be structured. It can't be done when the family is around, things are stressful or the radio is on. But as long as the environment is made comfortable, they can talk and they can give hugs and they can be very affectionate. But they have to know it's safe: they can't read their partner and don't know when it is okay to be physical. So the partner has to learn to say she would really like a hug. They will both need to learn to be open.'*

We have heard that before: people with Asperger's syndrome need a comfortable environment and need to feel safe. Which makes us consider: Maxine said earlier that most of her clients had jobs, but a workplace is not always a comfortable and safe environment. Maxine laughs and says: *'A lot of my clients are high earners! They are employed, and their work is within the area of their special interest. I have pilots as clients! They don't have to talk a lot to people to fly a plane. But when I talk to them, I find out they have always had an interest in planes. I have people working in the underground, or in the train service, who have always had an interest in trains or in IT or in engineering. As long as their vocation is within their interest, they can excel, because they will know everything.'*

Maxine's answer really surprises us, because we had heard that so many employers think it is difficult to have employees with Asperger's. In fact, we were told that only 15 per cent of the people with Asperger's syndrome in the UK can hold down a job. Although Maxine knows that this is the official percentage, she does have her doubts about the actual figure: *'I think it's a false statistic. The record only shows people that have "Asperger's" on their medical record. Those are the ones that are so obvious on the autism spectrum, they must have had an early diagnosis. The ones that have high-functioning autism often get missed. People that come to me for an assessment rarely put Asperger's on their medical record, and so do not figure in the statistics.'* Maxine's explanation does make sense. We ask her what she thinks will happen with employment now that more and more people are diagnosed with Asperger's. *'There are companies coming up now, IT and engineering companies for instance, who are specifically looking for people with Asperger's. They know that people with Asperger's know their stuff, are committed to the work and won't be spending time standing outside the room chatting to other people. They just get on with it. In fact, they make very desirable employees.'* That sounds like there is a good future for people coping with Asperger's syndrome. As Maxine said, with more support from the government, therapists, teachers, universities, from everyone, better understanding can be achieved. And with that understanding, there is no reason why people with Asperger's syndrome shouldn't have good relationships and hold down good jobs.

10.

ABOUT TRAINS, COMICS AND CUTBACKS

Elsbeth van de Ven is director of Beekmans and Van de Ven rehabilitation agency.

The Beekmans and Van de Ven rehabilitation agency helps people with difficulties in finding and keeping suitable work. Their speciality is rehabilitating people with psychological problems such as ADHD and ASD. The agency fields 18 professionals with a background in occupational health and safety, psychiatric care or special education. Elsbeth herself has a background in caring for people with learning difficulties. By now, the team has been reinforced with psychologists, career consultants, vocational experts and a job hunter.

Ten years ago, before starting her own company, Elsbeth was a job coach for the Cello Foundation, a care provider for people with a learning disability. She helped people find work. *'I counselled people with a mild learning disability. People who perform excellently when they are given the right instructions,'* Elsbeth says, when we have established ourselves at a large table in the meeting room of her office. *'The learning disability seemed to disappear if such was provided.'* After a brief silence she cautiously adds: *'But I cannot prove this. This is nothing more than my personal impression. It was not even very difficult to help these people find work. At first, we went looking for routine work, simple work, like photocopying papers. What they had to do was described in a schedule. But it soon turned out that they were able to do more. Light administrative work, for example. They had many more abilities than anybody could ever have suspected.'*

Her current partner, Leo Beekmans, also worked as a job coach at Cello. They were successful. It was a favourable job market. Companies cried out for good staff. Employers were granted subsidies to hire people receiving benefits under the Dutch Invalidity Insurance (Young Disabled Persons) Act. They even managed to help people from the day-care centre into paid jobs. People who had actually been written off before. *'That did cause a lot of resistance and fear,'* Elsbeth says. *'Especially from parents, carers and assistance workers. "Is he actually going to make it?" they wondered. But eventually, having work turns out to be a boon to them. It allows them to grow and it is excellent for their self-worth. That is a nice thing to see.'*

Elsbeth and Leo wanted to develop that idea. A new challenge lay ahead. They founded the Beekmans and Van de Ven rehabilitation agency. *'The demand was there. Many people with a disability wanted to get help in their quest for suitable work. We worked on behalf of the employment agencies. At a certain point we were also asked if we could help people with a normal IQ, but who continued to drop out, or could not start a training course or find work. This mainly concerned people who had been diagnosed with Asperger's syndrome or PDD-NOS. Sometimes these were very gifted people. We wondered: "How do we deal with this?" After some time, we found out how. Listen carefully and get to know these people well. Involve assistance workers, partners and parents to obtain as much information as possible about someone's character, and what this person needs to be able to perform well. Only then could we make things work. It is important to know what motivates them. What does such a person really like to do? You cannot get someone with autism to work in a garden centre if he is afraid to get his hands dirty. The social security organisation may well say that he has to take the job on offer, but then it is doomed to failure. It is also important to personally guide these people. We do not say: "Go and apply there." No, we accompany them to the interview. See how things go and help clarify certain matters.*

For the employer as well. Explain in what circumstances the person involved performs best. This was already our work method for people with learning difficulties. We were used to it. That approach also seems to work for people with ASD.'

We ask Elsbeth for examples. Elsbeth paints the picture of a somewhat older teacher at a college. She took him on as a client about ten years ago and she has learned a lot from him. We picture him in front of the class. Let's call him John. John teaches book-keeping. He has been divorced and has remarried. The school needs to reorganise. John is given a new position but it does not go well. He drops out and has burn-out. John keeps up appearances in front of his wife for another year. Every morning, he picks up his suitcase and his sandwich box, pretending to go to work. Eventually, John ends up at the unemployment agency and at his GP surgery. John is diagnosed with Asperger's syndrome. He now knows what's up with him. Trains, stations and timetables – these are things that fascinate John. He can become totally engrossed in them. An obvious ending to this tale would be for John to start working for a railway company, but this doesn't happen. It is clear, however, that he is very good at working with figures. Going back to teaching is not an option either. Teaching works as long as it is a one-way street. He is good at explaining his subject, but contact with the pupils is difficult, whereas that is exactly what is demanded of a teacher in the modern education system. He does not have patience with pupils who do not understand what he says. He cannot help pupils with problems properly. In a conversation with Elsbeth, John says: *'Everybody thinks that they are slightly autistic. Men clearly think that because they cannot empathise so well. But for me, it is a million times worse. For me, the world is total chaos. It takes a lot of energy for me to get everything straight and start a conversation with you. I see reactions that I cannot interpret. I hear ambiguity when you talk, and I really have to make an effort to understand what you say and how to process information.'* Eventually, his dexterity with figures is decisive.

Via a secondment agency John ends up as financial assistant at a production company, where his autism is taken into account. He is given a room of his own, as he cannot handle acoustic stimuli well. His supervisor and co-workers understand that he might react somewhat bluntly. After all, he does not come across as very friendly and jovial, but he means well. John is also provided with flexible working hours. When things have been very busy for a while, he can take extra days off to rest. That way, he is not troubled too much by stress. Everybody is content. A cordial friendship even develops between John and the company director.

'Another example?' Elsbeth asks. She is a good storyteller…so why not? This time our man is a social geographer. He started out at the lower school of agriculture and eventually graduated at Wageningen Agricultural University. He used to be the odd one out. *'He moves somewhat stiffly,'* Elsbeth says. We have an impression. Let's call him Hank. Hank is very formal, including his manner of dress. The top button of his shirt is always done up. He is very interested in maps and is well informed about all new highways that are built. He knows all the bicycle tracks by heart. As a child, Hank already used to draw maps. While he knows what he is talking about, he cannot find a job as he is unable to present himself well in interviews. Eventually he ends up in Switzerland via a project of the European Social Fund. He works hard there. He needs to map wildlife and skiing areas. But Hank also has a role as a pioneer and is expected to lobby for support. The work is very much project-based. He has to think carefully whom to address, when to address them, and what about. All this in a foreign country. At the same time he tries to make money as a pizza chef and tries his hand at drawing comic strips. We are not surprised that things get on top of him. Nor does it surprise us that, apart from ASD, he also has ADHD. Hank has a breakdown and returns to the Netherlands. He ends up at the unemployment agency but is not declared completely unfit for work. Hank does not want

to rely on benefit and starts working in a warehouse, working below his level. He is understimulated at this job, and does not like this at all. He wants more challenge in his work, preferably something in planning – something he has been trained for, after all. It doesn't go well. Again he ends up at a mental health institution, and is given a room in an assisted living project. Then Elsbeth enters the picture. She is requested to help him get a job that suits him better. He prefers to work for the municipality, but really is not suited for that. Such work would involve a lot of political games and you have to be able to lobby. Elsbeth is afraid that he will not make it there. So what are the possibilities? His dream is to have a good income and a house of his own and to make money drawing comic strips. Elsbeth thinks of the combination of IT and physical planning. She ends up at Falkplan, a company that draws maps. She calls the company and says: *'I have someone for you. He works in great detail and is highly accurate. He may have a somewhat slower work speed, but he is loyal and won't be off sick a single day. And you get a subsidy to boot.'* It works. By now, Hank has a fixed contract and a house of his own. His dream has come true for the most part. He still draws comics in his free time.

Elsbeth is employed by the benefit agency and municipalities to assist people on disability benefit, but also by companies requesting her to assist people who drop out. Under the Dutch law pertaining to rehabilitation from sick leave, the employer is obliged to make efforts to help sick people get back to work. Otherwise they have to pay. Beekmans and Van de Ven, in consultation with the people who drop out and the employer, looks for a suitable solution. This often means finding a new job, sometimes in the same company, sometimes somewhere else. It also happens that the employee takes the initiative. For example, an employee diagnosed with ASD might want help in preparing for a change in their work situation. Or the employee wants assistance in talking with his employer because he thinks that he doesn't receive sufficient support to perform well. *'In that case we sit down with the employer and explain what the employee can and cannot do,'* Elsbeth says. *'We then try to think of very practical solutions. People who have been diagnosed can receive financial support from the unemployment agency to enlist our aid, should they run the risk of dropping out. Sometimes the employer will have to pay for this.'*

There was a time when the job market was prospering and companies were crying out for personnel. The situation is quite different now. That is why it is harder to find jobs for people. But according to Elsbeth, there is yet another reason why the situation has become more difficult. *'Nowadays, much more demands are made of communicative and social skills. Consultation has become more important than it used to be. There is less well-defined work. That is often outsourced. A branch that is still going strong is the IT sector. Positions such as software testers or programmers. On the other hand, the people we guide sometimes have wishes that cannot be fulfilled. They say, for example, that they want to work with people in the social service sector. This may be feasible, provided they are properly instructed. Certain actions, such as washing people. As long as there are clear protocols.'* It reminds us of an article we read recently. That article said that a lot of routine jobs that nurses currently do, could be done by less highly trained people. That would give nurses more time to do work they do not have time for now, but which is actually very important in nursing. Elsbeth sees this as well. There are possibilities for people who want to be rehabilitated right there. *'People with ASD like doing that,'* she says, *'and they are not quickly distracted from it, so it would work well.'*

Elsbeth has a lot of contact with employers. What has changed in the last ten years? Is there more understanding for employees who have ASD? *'There is more understanding because it is better known. Everybody knows someone with ASD.'* But if cutbacks need to be made...? *'Yes, people often ask about this, but if someone performs well, having ASD is of no consequence. The fact is, however, that a problem occurs if the employee with autism has a lot of trouble adapting socially. For example, when they display claiming behaviour. They demand for their regular job consultant to be there for them, even if momentarily unavailable.'* Elsbeth drums her fingers on the table, so that we can get the idea. *'I need to talk to him right now because it concerns something important!'* she cries out. *'They don't understand that they have to wait. They don't accept that there are truths other than their own. The people who don't get that often don't make it. They become a nuisance to the other people in the organisation.'*

Beekmans and Van de Ven helps about 60 per cent of the people they counsel to find a job. *'However, there is a real difference for every person. If you are already at a certain age, have diplomas and work experience, it is a lot easier than when you don't. Although young people who are not yet trained sometimes get a job precisely because they can still be moulded.'* The home situation is taken into account when looking for suitable work. Many people with ASD and a family cannot work full-time. But Beekmans and Van de Ven does not provide any assistance at home. Elsbeth: *'We do take it into consideration, as we need to have a complete picture, but we are not family coaches.'*

Elsbeth describes the employee with ASD as *'loyal and motivated. They can discuss things in depth, pay attention to details, are accurate and can solve problems excellently. They can serve as an example for other people. They often do that accidentally. They are very honest and say what they think. They don't have ulterior motives and are therefore also very reliable. It is our experience that people with ASD can be helped to a job fairly easily.'* Elsbeth likes collaborating with people who have autism.

'Society has changed,' Elsbeth says when we ask her what she thinks is the reason why there are so many more people with autism of late. *'Take education, for example. In the past, a teacher stood in front of the class and told you what to do. Now you already have to keep your own workbook at kindergarten. That is very complicated for a child with autism. You are already being judged at an early age on social skills. These days, you have to be able to*

do several things simultaneously. At a certain point, problems arise and they end up on disability benefits.' That is true. But what is the solution? *'Special education,'* Elsbeth answers. But that is precisely the sector in which the purse strings will be tightened. *'I know. That is a very bad thing for children and young people with a learning difficulty. They miss the boat.'*

And adults with autism? *'You need to be able to do much more nowadays. A lot more demands are made on people. Personal skills, communicating, collaborating, gathering information quickly and skilfully, having a flexible mind, making the right choices between essential and unimportant things. All that is difficult for people with ASD. These demands are being made on a simple production worker. Positions are what they are, and are not adapted to people who may perform very well in a different manner. Employers should be more aware of that.'* But employers want to make a profit. *'That's right. But a profit can also be made if you are flexible and adapt positions so you can hire good, loyal people with ASD for your company. Each position is now easily assigned six various competencies the applicant needs to meet – and is hired or rejected on. People with ASD excel in some of these competencies; they are better than all the others. But they have a lower score on other competencies. Why not look at these competencies from a creative point of view and create new positions for which you hire experts? You are then giving people with ASD a chance.'* We get it. Employers should have a more 'out-of-the-box' way of thinking. But do they have the right competencies for that? As far as Elsbeth is concerned, large companies should be required by law to hire people with learning disabilities. At least for a minimum percentage of the workforce. But, given current Dutch government policy, it's doubtful whether this would happen. It is certain, however, that considerable cuts will be made in assistance to people with an intellectual disability . The government intends to eliminate a quarter of the 20,000 benefit agency jobs. People just have to apply via the internet, or so government argues. The benefit agencies' budget is being reduced by one third. That has consequences for helping people with autism to find a job. For Elsbeth it means that she cannot work in the same way as she used to. *'If you can spend more time on proper assistance for people with ASD, you can ensure that they end up in a good place. We only start with rehabilitation if we know someone's wishes and abilities and what work conditions are necessary. You need to find that out first. If you don't and start mediating right away, this will lead to job placements failing more often, causing more people to claim benefits in the end. It is already the case that people with ASD who are on unemployment benefits cannot call in aid from a rehabilitation agency. In the end, you pay the price.'* If cuts need to be made, Elsbeth thinks it would be better to aim for more efficient cooperation between organisations that focus on rehabilitation, such as mental health institutions, local governments, benefit agencies and the rehabilitation agencies. *'I think that if we collaborate and make a proper division of tasks, there is a lot to be gained.'*

11.

'IMPOSSIBLE DOESN'T EXIST, IMPOSSIBLE AT THIS MOMENT DOES'

Barbara de Leeuw (44) is an autism coach and educationalist. She has her own practice. She helps people deal with ASD in the family and at work. Her son has ASD and Gilles de la Tourette syndrome. Her other son has PDD-NOS and ADHD. Barbara has been diagnosed with ADHD. When we speak to her, the ASD diagnosis has been confirmed by a psychiatrist.

'Good morning! Look at the sun shining again! *dances for joy*' Barbara de Leeuw tweets cheerfully as we make our way to see her. Once we are at her home in Rotterdam she says enthusiastically that she would also like to write a positive book on autism. *'But my book will be more about the educational and practical side,'* she says. *'How do you get to the point where you can call yourself successful? It isn't about a house of your own and a top position at a company. It is about being able to perform satisfactorily. And this also applies to someone who is in a supervised residential arrangement and works as a volunteer on a special care farm.'*[1] Or to an educationalist with an autism agency of her own.

Barbara has ADHD. That has been established. But as far as she is concerned, that doesn't quite cover it all. *'I always feel restless,'*

---

1   A special care farm is a farm where people who need care can live and work. They look after animals or work in the flower gardens.

she explains. *'Hyperactivity. My restlessness is inside. I always feel like I need to rush for the train. And my head that just keeps on thinking. But there is more.'* Something which is also confirmed by her son's psychologists. They actually think she is more autistic than a person with ADHD. Barbara is rather oversensitive to stimuli. *'Especially to sound. People all talking at the same time. After this conversation I'll be exhausted. But images, too. Just walking around on the streets is overstimulating. All these people shooting past each other. I can come home from grocery shopping and feel deadbeat. When I am that tired, my information processing is much slower. Even a simple question like "Would you like a cup of coffee?" can become hard to understand. At such times, I can really only do one thing at the time.'* She takes medication – antidepressants – and she occasionally steals half a tablet of Ritalin from her son. She has done this before our conversation. *'Very little, but just enough to make my voice a little calmer,'* she laughs.

Barbara has two sons. Her eldest son has a *'crackling compulsive disorder,'* is Barbara's name for it. A classic case of autism and Tourette syndrome. That is a neuropsychiatric disorder characterised by tics. Although Barbara's son does not have ADHD, it is remarkable that 60 per cent of people with Tourette syndrome do also have ADHD. The combination with PDD-NOS is very common as well. He lives in a psychiatric treatment centre. His little brother has ADHD and PDD-NOS. *'He really takes after his mother,'* Barbara says.

In 2007 Barbara founded her agency. That year, she moved to another town. *'A good time to start something new,'* she says. She is a volunteer at Humanitas, one of the main social services and community building organisations in the Netherlands. She, by herself, set up the Humanitas Home Administration project. Prior to that, she had several jobs, working as an executive secretary and management assistant. In the meantime, she completed a degree in education studies. She can combine her work well with caring for her children. For her current work it is an advantage that, because of her sons, she already knows a lot about autism and ADHD. Barbara: *'Having studied education studies and my experience as a hands-on expert are what set things in motion. I started with educational support and later added information provision, workshops and trainings. Now, I mainly coach adults with ASD or parents of children with ASD. I work about 20 hours per week. I can't do more. When I give a workshop, I am unable to work for at least 24 hours after. I cannot have more than five or six clients either.'* For her coaching work, Barbara visits people at home. This might involve having to tell adults who have just been diagnosed with ASD what it entails and how to deal with it. She also visits schools to inform teachers about how to handle children with ADHD or ASD, often in a very practical manner. Based on the child's behaviour, she teaches them to see when a child is overstimulated, and what action to take. *'I now also visit a family where several people have ASD,'* Barbara says. *'That is an obstacle to communication. Then I have to ensure that they are all singing from the same sheet.'* She really enjoys her work.

Barbara calls her ADHD and ASD her *'talents'*. Isn't that a little strange? *'No it isn't. Everybody is always talking about agony. I just call it top-class sport. Maybe I have a very positive disposition. It's no fun if you can't do lots of things in the time you would like to be able to. For example, I can't extend my practice and at the same time keep my house clean and take my children to the swimming pool once in a while. That is annoying but I have accepted it by now. I also get many positive things from it. I am very good at out-of-the-box thinking and I have good analytical skills. That's very useful in my work. When I go somewhere, I am able to make out quite quickly what's going right, what's going wrong, and what needs to be done. I could never have done my job so well if I didn't have autism. But my ADHD is meaningful as well. I hear and I see everything. I register everything. It very occasionally happens that I am off target and focus, for example, too much on a detail, which subsequently appears not to be so important. Sometimes the penny only drops in the middle of the night, making me wake up with a start.'* Again Barbara's contagious laugh is heard in the living room.

How did Barbara notice that she was different from other people? *'I wet my bed until I was 15-years-old. The first time I got through the night and stayed dry, my mother all but sank to her knees from gratitude. My motor skills were a disaster. Other children had extra lessons in mathematics at secondary education, but I had gymnastics coaching. I felt that I didn't fit in. They thought I was lazy, cheeky and sharp. It was always negative. And I didn't get it, because I meant well. I thought, I can't be the bitch they all say I am, can I? But I couldn't explain it. And that was the worst part to me. I only had one girlfriend and she was weird as well. Birds of a feather flock together. Still. In my circle of friends, everybody has something. I sometimes find it difficult to live in a subculture of persons with autism and ADHD. We are a minority. I was once at a training where only three people were present: the trainer, me and another person. I didn't fit in at all and had no rapport with the other two. Later it almost made me cry.'*

Barbara wonders if she is still able to perform at all in the world of the neurotypicals, the 'ordinary' people. She used to adapt but finds this becoming increasingly difficult. She doesn't feel she belongs there. She has the feeling that people are looking at her and thinking that there is something wrong with her. Other mothers in the school yard, for example. She can't put into words exactly what these people see in her. Her husband, Cor, who is reading the newspaper on the other side of the room, comes to her rescue: *'She may be very startled. If a conversation suddenly takes a different turn from what Barbara expects, it frightens her. She then adopts a defensive attitude. When, in the supermarket, the girl behind the counter unexpectedly asks if she wants coupons, Barbara is confused.'* As long as everything goes as Barbara expects, there is no problem. But she isn't good at anticipating the unexpected. She does pick up the thread again, but needs a little time.

'I was the explosive one, the hyper girl, the fuss maker,' Barbara continues her story about her childhood. *'That's what they said about me, but to my way of thinking I was always in a dream world. I sometimes missed entire episodes. I could be taken to school in the*

morning and collected in the afternoon without being able to say what had happened in the meantime. I still have that. I can drive by car from A to B without knowing the route I took. To others I was apparently very boisterous. I could not in fact imagine that. As far as talking is concerned, I can. I can talk the hind leg off a donkey.' She also speaks as if she is in a hurry, we notice. *'And to think I took half a tablet of Ritalin just now,'* she laughs. *'Just imagine how things would have been otherwise. It helps me to keep my voice a little calmer and to contain my impulsiveness. Otherwise I continue saying all kinds of things, all the time; I associate like crazy.'*

At primary school Barbara was not bullied, mainly thanks to a teacher whom she would like to proclaim the best in the Netherlands. But she didn't really fit in either. Allowance was made for her. Things were quite different at secondary school. There, Barbara spent her entire breaks cooped up in the toilets to avoid social interaction with fellow students, for fear of being bullied. She went to a Dalton school, a type of education that emphasises the student's freedom of choice, collaboration with other students and the development of independence. It didn't work for Barbara. She had to repeat the fourth year of secondary education, and the following year derailed completely. She lacked the independence to do assignments. In the end, she didn't finish secondary education. At age 17, Barbara left her parental home. *'A row with my parents,'* she explains. She doesn't want to say much about it. Barbara lived with a foster family for a year, and was then placed in a supervised residential arrangement. But the supervision didn't amount to much. *'This supervisor came by once every three months and we then gave him a list of things in the house that needed repair. A new washing machine and a new ironing board would then be provided. I really had the time of my life there. I was living on social security and I had joined the new wave scene. It's called gothic nowadays. I had a Mohican black as the night and walked around in a long, black coat with red lining. I slept from early in the morning until five in the afternoon and then quickly went to the supermarket to pick up a bag of potatoes and a jar of mayonnaise. After dinner I went to the youth centre again, where I spent the night. We then ate sandwiches, drank tea and occasionally smoked a joint.'* So Barbara had already settled into a subculture there as well. A pleasant environment with people who accepted her as she was. *'Everybody there was a little weird and strange,'* she says. *'That was allowed.'* Barbara still goes to a Celtic music festival with Cor once in a while and tends to dress like a hippy.

Later on, Barbara finished intermediate business education within one year. She made herself obtain a diploma, and therefore made many sacrifices and worked hard. And she met her first husband, with whom she was to be in a 20-year relationship and with whom she had her two children. During this time she flitted from one job to the other. Many administrative positions. But in these positions Barbara was expected to show deference and do what the boss said. That is exactly where things did not always go right. *'I didn't know my place. If I thought my boss wasn't doing his job well, I just told him so. I just said he was mucking about. Or I would be taking minutes at meetings and start interfering in the discussion. Often I would suddenly come up with solutions for problems that were being discussed, but that was of course unacceptable. I was only a typist.'* She starts laughing out loud. *'I didn't understand at all that this was not done.'* But how did people react to it? *'Well, dismissal,'* she says. *'I have a four-page CV.'* Misunderstandings at work that gave her pause for thought happened quite often. *'I once had a job at a lawyer's office. I had to type letters that had been recorded on a dictaphone. It was part-time work, three days per week. At some point there was not enough work and people had to go. A choice had to be made between me – a part-time mother with two small children who very often had to take time off for conversations with support workers and school – and a girl in her early twenties who worked full-time there. The choice fell on me. I understood, but that girl was angry that I had to leave and therefore she left as well. As did another colleague. All of a sudden there were two vacancies. I didn't understand that I still stood a chance of staying there. I didn't even present myself. The lawyer I worked for even asked the director why he didn't keep me on. He then said: "She has not shown at all that she wants to." It hadn't occurred to me at all, either, that I should have done that. So again I had lost my job.'* Shortly afterwards Barbara moved to Rotterdam and started her own agency. She is her own boss now and quite likes it. And she has passed the magic age limit of 40. *'I love having passed 40,'* she says. *'I am no longer considered an annoying child or a strange adolescent, or a young adult who thinks she knows it all. Up to the age of 40, I had the feeling that people underestimated me. When now I say that I know something, people accept it. When now I act strangely, I am all of a sudden a cool bit of skirt. And there is nothing I ought, should, must do any more. If I don't feel like something, I say so. If I think it is too busy, I send people home. Isn't it awesome? It probably also has to do with my work,'* she says, putting things in perspective. *'In the past, I had my say in circumstances where I would have done better not to. Now, I am invited for my knowledge of autism and I am appreciated.'*

Barbara gets some fresh coffee and tea. *'Without spilling,'* she notes with some pride. She lights another cigarette while we ask the next question. Would she have liked to be diagnosed with autism and ADHD as a child? *'Yes,'* she says immediately. *'What I missed as a child was an understanding coach. Someone who could have done for me what I now do for others. Who makes the link with this other world and helps to understand it. Someone who helps people with autism develop themselves in our society to the greatest extent possible. I always say: "Impossible doesn't exist, but impossible at this moment does." The fact that something is not possible now doesn't mean that it will always be so.'* Barbara thinks that children and young people with autism are pampered too much. *'I often hear parents say: "He can't do that because he has autism." Or: "Leave him be, he is autistic." Do you think that I could have developed myself into an independent autism coach and could have run a family if I had been pampered? I did miss the understanding and the explanation. I simply had to overcome my behaviour. No reasons were given. I didn't have a clue. I would like to have had that coaching. The potential of people with autism could certainly be considered more, instead of overprotecting them due to their disabilities.'*

A colleague of Barbara, Marjon Kuipers, has thought up the 'Autism-friendly' initiative. Barbara supports that initiative. Companies and organisations can follow a training from Marjon in which they learn to consider clients who are autistic. If they have followed the training and they have the right intentions, they are awarded the 'Autism-friendly' certificate. Marjon is successful and trains all sorts of people, from mortgage advisors to owners of a driving-school. Thirty-one companies have already availed themselves of her services. In Rotterdam Barbara can't get the project off the ground. She doesn't have the right contacts in the business community. And what about a hallmark for autism-friendly schools? *'That would be nice,'* Barbara says, *'but it is hard to realise. The regular education systems don't dare do it because then they will not just get a certificate, but a brand. And next, they will get too many children with autism. They cannot handle that.'*

According to the Australian autism expert Tony Attwood[2] (Barbara: *'Mister Autism himself'*), there are more women with autism who haven't been diagnosed than men. He claims that the ratio is one woman to two men with autism, while up to now it has been assumed that only one in five people with an ASD is female. Attwood thinks that women are better able than men to camouflage their social handicap. What are hands-on expert Barbara's thoughts on this? *'I think that he is right. Women are by nature more social. They have more empathy and are more emotional. Men do not have to be social as far as we are concerned. They are allowed to be quiet and a little rude. Men with an ASD become rigid and are less approachable. Women suffer more from processing stimuli and become tired more quickly. It is noticeable in boys that all of a*

---

2   Tony Attwood is the author of several books on Asperger's syndrome. His book, *Asperger's Syndrome: A Guide for Parents and Professionals,* provides information on diagnosis, problems of social relations, sensory issues, motor control and other typical issues which face people with Asperger's and their support networks. Visit www. tonyattwood.com.eu

sudden they can have inexplicable tantrums and become aggressive, while girls bottle it up more and are introverted. The latter is of course less noticeable.' So ASD may lead to different symptoms in men and women. Symptoms that are less noticeable in women than in men. That could be a good explanation, but we do not know for sure.

We ask the unavoidable last question: does Barbara consider herself successful? *'Yes,'* she answers wholeheartedly. Why? *'Because I am leading a life that I feel very comfortable with.'*

12.

'IF IT'S IN MY INTEREST,
I WILL TELL'

Dominiek Heyvaert (45) has known for seven years that he has ASD. He was born and raised in the Flemish town of Merchtem, near Brussels. Dominiek lives there by himself, in the former parental home. His sister lives next door. He works for the Inland Revenue Services.

We come into contact with Dominiek Heyvaert through a remarkable Flemish website[1] – an initiative by a group of people with normal competence who have ASD. If you need to make contact with an autistic person, that's where you could go. Dominiek is the website's moderator. We emailed him with our request to make contact with Flemish people with autism, so that we could conduct our interviews. Dominiek returned ten positive responses. 'And,' he wrote in an email, 'I also want to collaborate on the book myself.' We agree to meet him at home in Merchtem. On the cosy terrace of Passerel Inn, situated beside the canal surrounding the church, we get to know him well: a man who has come to know his boundaries and has learned how to lead a happy and sociable life within them.

Dominiek was 38-years-old when he was diagnosed with autism. Changing personal circumstances revealed his autism to him. His mother died. After some time, his father met another woman, with whom he went to live in another town. Dominiek

---

1   The flemish website is no longer available. All activities go via www. autismevlaanderen.be You can also contact the founders via email: renanautist@gmail.com

continued to live alone in the parental home, next door to his sister, three years his junior, who had been living for a number of years with her family in his grandfather's house. After a while Dominiek found that he missed the structure of family life. He neglected practical matters, although it didn't seem so bad to begin with. *'I learned to wash clothes from my father,'* Dominiek says. *'I divided ironing duty between my uncles and aunts.'* (A paternal uncle of his still lives in Merchtem, and four of his mother's six siblings also still live in the town. All highly convenient for Dominiek.) *'I have also learned to cook,'* he continues. *'Rice, potatoes or spaghetti, all that is no problem.'* But because Dominiek works full-time for the Inland Revenue Services, he often eats in a restaurant or bistro in the afternoon. It's not cheap. If he does cook, there is little variation. *'Cleaning the house was also do-able,'* he continues. *'But what eventually proved to be the last straw was the fact that I bought a compost container to put vegetable waste and leftovers in.'* Not a bad idea, if it weren't for the fact that Dominiek doesn't have a garden. What does he want with compost? *'I didn't realise something was wrong. My father pointed this out to me, and together we emptied out the compost container.'* The content was put in garbage bags, which Dominiek was to take to the recycling facility. But that didn't happen. He left the garbage bags in his garage, where after a while they started attracting rats. *'I saw the rats, but didn't make the link between them and the garbage in the bags.'* Fortunately, his sister did. The waste was put out for collection and the rats were caught.

A child of a friend of Dominiek's stepmother also has ASD. The similarities between this child's behaviour and Dominiek's made the child's parents decide to call the autism helpline. They requested an information pack on autism and passed it on to Dominiek. The pack also contained the book *Autisme verteld (Autism Explained)*. Dominiek read this book and recognised a lot of the symptoms in himself, leading him to want an assessment as soon as possible. A few months later he was diagnosed. Dominiek reads a lot about autism. *'I have read all the books about autism that are in the library,'* he says. *'Bit by bit the pieces of the puzzle came together. I could better place a number of things that had gone wrong – for example, that I am insensitive to smells. This occurs in people with autism. It all has to do with your senses. You are oversensitive to some stimuli, and to other stimuli you are undersensitive or have no sensation at all. I don't feel cold either. When you asked me at the start of the interview if I wanted to sit inside because it was still too nippy, I answered that it didn't matter to me. I don't feel the cold.'* Not being able to smell his own body odour actually embarrassed Dominiek once. During a trip to Norway, about ten years ago, he forgot to take his deodorant. He bought a new one, but it was a roll-on instead of the spray can that he is used to. After returning home, he didn't notice that the roller had dried out at some point and did not work any more. He continued using it. It was the height of summer, and consequently his colleagues at work, especially the women, started complaining. He was put on the spot by his immediate supervisor, who asked him to take better care of his personal hygiene. Dominiek is now able to laugh about what happened to him then. It will not happen again in a hurry. He did avoid his colleagues at work – especially the female ones – for a time, though.

In the 1970s, when Dominiek was attending primary school, autism was largely unknown. (Autism at the time was only diagnosed in combination with 'slow learning', as it was then called.) Dominiek experienced no trouble in primary school. He did go to a rehabilitation centre to improve his motor skills, and had speech therapy. *'The latter did not help sufficiently. This is a controversial issue nowadays. People think that it is not much use giving children with autism speech therapy. The communication problems are not linked to the pronunciation, but much more to understanding words and non-verbal communication. I now manage to read body language. You teach yourself in time. When you are young, you don't know how to behave properly if you have ASD.*

But later on, you learn to copy the behaviour you observe in others. You learn tricks.'

Dominiek had the advantage of growing up in a very sociable environment. His father and mother, like his many uncles and aunts, were very active in local associations. His mother was a board member of the local Catholic Working Women's society, and his father was secretary of the Catholic Workers Movement. His parents often took him along to social events, where he was always known as 'the Heyvaert boy'. *As a consequence I was accepted quickly, despite my limitations. People could see that something was wrong with me, but they couldn't pinpoint what it was. If, for example, I was helping to set up the room for the society's annual party, I usually didn't know where to start. There were so many tasks, such as arranging chairs, setting tables with plates, knives, forks, spoons and glasses, that I couldn't decide for myself where to help. Now that people know that I have autism, they tell me what to do.'* It was not long before Dominiek followed in his parents' footsteps and became a Catholic Workers Youth member. The people he got to know there are in his circle of friends. Many of them have now joined the Catholic Workers Movement, together with him. He is also very active as a volunteer worker. Apart from his activities for the Catholic Workers Movement, PASS (a self-help group run by and for young adults with autism) and Rent-an-autist, he works at the *Vredeseilanden*[2] a development aid organisation and at the fair-trade shop.

Dominiek likes to travel. As a volunteer for *Vredeseilanden* he went to Senegal to visit projects. That is where he acquired his taste for travel. Trips to Indonesia and Morocco and other places followed. He usually travels with groups from Govaka, the Catholic Workers Movement's travel organisation. But is travelling for people with autism really that easy? You may be faced with strange situations, after all. Dominiek doesn't want

---

2   Vredeseilanden is active within Sustainable Agricultural Chain Development. Their aim is to enable organisations of smallholder family farmers to successfully participate within sustainable value chains. Visit www. veco-ngo.org

that. That is why he usually travels with the same organisation. *The advantage of travelling with travel organisations is that everything is structured. You know the programme beforehand. If you go for a bike ride or walk, you know you will go from A to B that day. You are on the move for the entire day. When I went to Morocco, I had just been diagnosed. I had not told the tour guide that I have autism. After the flight from Brussels to Marrakech, we continued our journey by bus on the second day. We had to sit in the bus the entire day. I was very tired and was looking out of the window while the tour leader sat next to me and tried to make contact with me. I wasn't really aware of that. In the evening at the overnight place, I immediately arranged my sleeping place and sat down for a little while in the drawing room, with a book on autism. I was sitting alone to calm down and avoid stimuli, but the others joined me and asked me what the book I was reading was about. I explained it and said that I had autism.'* Dominiek laughs. *'The tour guide also heard this and immediately understood why I had been so silent during the bus trip. The penny dropped right away. He was a social assistant himself, so he knew something about autism. He understood that I was overstimulated by the trip.'* That was a lesson for Dominiek. *'I won't say straightaway in the company of strangers that I have autism. But during such a trip it is important that the tour guide knows. If I know that it may be in my interest, I will tell.'*

He wants to obtain a bookkeeping degree but this is a path of trial and error. *'At college I had a 90 per cent score for bookkeeping,'* Dominiek says, *'but I prefer to say nothing about the other subjects.'* After the first year he had a talk with the school's principal, who told him that although he would be allowed to continue his studies, his chance of success was practically nil. Dominiek started attending evening classes because the principal thought his chance of success was greater there. Dominiek managed to conclude his studies successfully via the evening classes.

Dominiek applied for a job and needed to sit a written test and present himself for an interview. He had no problem whatsoever with the written part, but as soon as the interview started, he got into trouble. He finds non-verbal communication and eye contact difficult. *'But,'* he says, *'when we are chatting as we are now, things go very well. However, as soon as you ask a question I don't expect, it takes longer for me to have an answer ready. Then I come across as not very easy-going.'* Dominiek cannot help this, of course, but he still is judged on the matter. After a one-year temporary contract he ended up unemployed, but fortunately not for long. The father of one of his sister's friends, who works at the Ministry of Finance, told him that the ministry was looking for people. Dominiek applied and on the strength of his letter, was hired as a contract civil servant. In order to obtain civil servant status within the Inland Revenue Services and advance in his career, he sat for exams several times. He noticed time and again that his limitations in oral skills constituted a problem. *'The written part went well, but I didn't score well on the oral part.'*

This changed when he was diagnosed with autism. First and foremost, it helped because the Belgian federal government had pledged to have 3 per cent of the workforce consist of people with special needs. When you are completing your CV, SELOR (the federal government's selection agency) offers you the opportunity to be entered in to the register of people with special needs. But what '(reasonable) adaptations' do you need to indicate when your disability is autism? For people who are in a wheelchair or who are blind, this is very obvious and adaptations are easy to apply for. But what adaptations does an autistic person need? For a start, if he chooses to take the opportunity of asking for an adaptation, he can only state 'autism spectrum disorder'. For the written exam he was allowed to sit in a separate room. *'This is good in itself,'* Dominiek says, *'but that is not really a problem for me.'* For the oral part, however, they did not take his disability into account at all, whereas that is what he was having difficulties with. He was to sit the exam on Friday afternoon at 2pm, but he was kept waiting for an hour. Precisely that week, Dominiek was to go away for the weekend with some friends. He was really stressed out, and failed. The next time he was better able to specify his problems. To indicate the problems he experiences during oral tests, he noted down: 'need more time for answering questions orally; problems understanding and showing non-verbal communication (eye contact)'. To be on the safe side, during the oral test he mentioned that he had autism and what problems this might cause during the interview. To his surprise the panel stated they had not been aware beforehand that he was on the special register.

This time Dominiek passed. Just after he was told that he had passed, Dominiek found an article on the Passwerk company in a staff magazine. This company seconds people with autism, mainly software testers (see Chapter 14). This article said something that annoyed Dominiek. *'It said that people with autism are mentally retarded and that the group of autistics contains few people with normal ability. That is more or less what it boiled down to.'* Dominiek was annoyed and wrote to the editor, albeit feeling a little anxious. As his statutory appointment was not yet finalised, he didn't want to tread on someone's toes. He had his supervisor read his letter first and decided to make a few adjustments. His letter contained a well substantiated overview of expert proof to the contrary of what the article said. The letter was published. As a result, the people at the selection agency, who had forgotten to pass on that he had ASD, gave him an apology.

Dominiek is aware that he is lucky to have been taught social skills at home. He doesn't need to be afraid of becoming isolated, but he does notice this threat to other people with autism. *'I get involved in things quite easily. If I join something, I am involved in the organisation within a year. Don't ask me how I do that. It probably has something to do with my upbringing. It's a shame that people with autism are quickly judged unable to fit in. Too little effort is then made to help these people perform better, and to involve them more. The qualities, the things that people with autism can do, are not sufficiently taken into consideration. They sooner look at the things people can't do. In my circle of acquaintances of people with autism, some have gone a long way. But if they receive insufficient support from their environment, they cannot perform well.'* At the same time, Dominiek thinks that people with ASD should talk more about their limitations. There first needs to be understanding, before support can be offered in a meaningful way. And that is exactly what Rent-an-autist is about.

13.

THE INVISIBLE
WHEELCHAIR

Karin Berman (49) is married and has a 25-year-old daughter. Karin works as careers advisor and autism coach for R95, a rehabilitation and care agency with branch locations all over the country, which helps people with a disability and /or difficulties finding a job. The autism team diagnosed Karin with Asperger's syndrome seven years ago.

We meet up with Karin in the town of Meppel (The Netherlands). The moment we come in, we can already see that she is doing well. She radiates self-confidence and laughs. But the road she travelled to get to where she is now was long, full of obstacles and beset by ignorance. She did not understand herself either. But now, after so many years, she dares to say with conviction that she is a successful autistic. ' I look at myself as a worthy human being, despite my limitations.'

Only after her study to become a career coach did things look up for Karin. She says: *'The benefit agency gave me permission to follow the part-time Personnel and Work training, to be trained as a career counsellor. I completed the training despite a number of problems. Sometimes I made mistakes when I thought I had understood the assignment I was given. I failed to understand the gist of conversations and didn't know why. I had trouble planning and keeping an overview. These are all problems I also encountered when I wanted to set up an information centre for career development, after having completed this training. I needed to do a lot of lobbying. The conversations didn't go well. When I came in, people were enthusiastic.*

When I left, they would say: 'We will be in touch'. I didn't understand what was going wrong. Finally, I came to the conclusion that something in my subconscious must be sabotaging me. Unconscious motives often play a big role in problems. During the rehabilitation course I ended up taking, I went to look for an agency that focused specifically on these matters.'

Karin suspected she was suffering from characteristics of the autism spectrum, and said so to the people at the rehabilitation agency. *'They asked if I had ever had myself assessed. I hadn't. I had characteristics. That was it. I had mentioned my suspicion of having autism once or twice during therapy, but then they said: "You? Not at all, you are so communicative!"'* On the advice of the agency Karin had herself assessed by the autism team and was diagnosed with Asperger's. Finally, everything made sense and Karin could start processing the past and look for the right assistance. That is how she ended up with her current employer, R95, a rehabilitation and care agency specialising in dealing with autism.

Karin's greatest fear was that she would prove unsuitable for a job as a careers advisor. Acknowledging non-verbal communication is difficult for her. During an internship at the agency she discovered that communication wasn't that difficult for her in a one-to-one setting. *'The main thing lacking at the time was self-confidence,'* Karin says. After a year and a half she plucked up the courage to sign a contract for a job as a careers advisor. Her work consisted of doing career assessments. Together with clients she made overviews of their weak and strong points, their interests and motivations, what they would need at their workplace and what they would like to do. Quite a lot of factors that require a considerable amount of empathy (not exactly one of the strongest points of people with ASD). Or have we got this wrong? Karin starts laughing and says: *'Well, I think the situation is somewhat different. It's not a question of empathy so much as powers of observation. I don't (or hardly) perceive what people feel. Consequently, it's difficult for me to empathise. If you are sad and I don't notice, I can't take that into consideration either.'* When we ask her if she has learned to recognise non-verbal communication, her answer is no. *'That cannot be learned.'* We look at her in astonishment. So Karin performs well while missing an important part of communication? *'I do observe some body language. I see, for example, that you are laughing right now. But I don't perceive the nuances expressed in your face.'* We don't yet fully understand. Is Karin able to perform successfully because she has developed mechanisms of her own to compensate for this 'deficiency'? She explains: *'To clients without autism I say beforehand that I do not perceive body language. I also ask them to be very explicit and say clearly what is bothering them, and indicate when I say something wrong. My style of communication is very direct, as a result of which my communication skills are actually very strong in certain respects. In addition, I have been trained well in discussion techniques. By asking questions I receive a lot of information. I also listen carefully to people, so I can distil the essence of what they say. Pitch and choice of words are important indicators to me. For me, language is much more multifaceted than for most people. For you, it is not so important what synonym you use for a word. It all means the same. That doesn't apply to me. Words can be very similar, but sometimes the nuance is just slightly different.'*

Karin guides clients both with and without ASD. She has Asperger's herself. Is this an advantage when helping autistic people? *'Absolutely,'* she answers. *'It is often said that people with autism cannot put themselves in other people's shoes. But, between ourselves, on the contrary, we are very good at it. We have a common view of the world and frame of reference. Two words are enough for us. So yes, I can empathise properly with people with autism. Often, they feel understood by someone for the first time in their lives. That has a big impact.'* Karin provides insight into autism. What is autism? What does it mean for that person? How do I deal with it? Karin: *'I teach these people to understand themselves better, and give them advice. I discuss what they can do in case of overstimulation. I am bothered by this quite a lot myself, but by now I am able to handle it. That is why I only work 12 hours a week and sleep for a few hours in the afternoon. I travel first class on the way home from work. I take the lift instead of the stairs. The fact is that in my case exercise causes overstimulation.'*

She tells the story of a woman who had persistent tantrums of anger. *'That ruined her life. In the past, she even attempted suicide a number of times. Therapists didn't understand her. They said that she had better get a grip on these attacks, but could not tell her how. I started to work with her and looked at everything from the viewpoint of overstimulation. Then she understood. She has now organised her life and living environment differently, and is mostly able to prevent the attacks. She has, furthermore, given advice to the people who counsel her. She taught them how to deal with her overstimulation. They can't expect her to look for help in the middle of a tantrum. Impossible. When you are overstimulated you can't think, find words or take action. You are totally paralysed.'*

Karin is a coach, but also receives support herself from several coaches. She sees a therapist from the autism team who helps her to monitor the main events in her life. She sees this therapist once every two months. *'Then we talk about my work, my relationship, the household, motherhood and health. Where is there room for adjustment?'* Karin also has a job coach, a manager from R95. This woman guides Karin in day-to-day issues at work. *'Because she knows the company and my clients, she is quickly able to adjust whatever needs adjusting, which comes in very handy.'* Officially, they meet once a fortnight. But Karin can always drop in on her. *'That is a real necessity,'* Karin says. *'I find a lot of things difficult at work. For example, I always make a report of each client discussion. That report needs to be stored in a file. Things go wrong with these tabs and loops. It used to take me a quarter of an hour to file a page. Now I put the report in a tray and others file it. That is much more efficient. From a practical point of view, so many things can be adjusted at work. That is the good thing. But one's employer and colleagues do need to be receptive to it. It's also necessary to have a clear overview of the problems. If it turns out that someone is bothered by all the talking going on in the work environment, that person can be provided with earplugs, an MP3-player or a separate workstation, for example.'* Karin's third coach visits to help out with practical matters: putting things in order, doing odd jobs, helping with administration. *'She takes over the things I cannot do. I can clean the toilet, for example, but I am totally beat afterwards. This has to do with keeping an overview and the amount of stimuli I receive.'*

Karin now knows how to handle her autism. She is helped by her coaches. But how was it in the past? *'I went to and from school by bicycle. Once I got home, I had a headache, every day. Now I know that this has to do with overstimulation. I also had tantrums at the end of the day. Around dinnertime I started screaming and slamming doors. I didn't want to eat any more. If I was forced to, I calmed down. Eating has always been my anchor in life. I always wanted to know what we would eat tomorrow, and the day after, and the day after that. Now I know that these tantrums are also linked to overstimulation. I received all these impressions, all day long. At the end of the day, I couldn't process them any more. The bucket was full. My brain would short-circuit. Everything was released in a tantrum that had nothing to do with anger.'*

At primary school things went well in the sense that Karin had no problem dealing with the subject material. She didn't need to make an effort, and even got bored. She obtained a very high score on the final aptitude test. She went to grammar school but later on fell back to the level of general secondary education. *'Thanks to the teachers, I obtained my diploma. One of them said: "You didn't finish your paper, but if you had, it would certainly have been an A. That's why you only get a D." That was enough to pass.'* We laugh. That's one way to graduate. But things were not easy for Karin at secondary school. She suffered a lot from headaches. She had difficulty concentrating, and she was bullied. During that time Karin saw various psychologists and psychiatrists, but they didn't discover anything unusual. After secondary school, Karin embarked on various trainings, but did not finish a single one. She entered the job market unskilled, and had many odd jobs. She worked in manufacturing and catering. Later on, she landed herself a job as layout assistant in a printing office, but that position was made redundant after the digitalisation of production processes. Karin next took up senior secondary vocational education at the vocational school for women, following which she was offered a job in the Immigration Service. After six months, her contract was not renewed. *'I asked a lot of questions. I wanted to do a good job, but my boss interpreted this as lacking independence.'* She was forced to live on unemployment benefit. And it didn't end there, as her husband suffered a heart attack. *'He meant everything to me. I loved him, he gave me structure and security. He mainly looked after our daughter and did the housekeeping. All of a sudden, there was the risk that I might lose him. I was afraid of going on by myself. I couldn't handle that. Fortunately, my husband survived the heart attack.'*

Karin had a mental breakdown. She ended up on sickness benefit and had to go into psychotherapeutic day care for four years, followed by five more years of follow-up treatment. Over these years she was given various diagnoses. The first psychiatrist she saw was of the opinion that she was suffering from borderline personality disorder. The second thought she had an anxiety-compulsive disorder, while the third stuck to post-traumatic stress disorder with aspects of borderline. Once again, a whole flock of therapists put in their two pennyworth. But it didn't occur to anyone that Karin's problems might be linked to autism. *'A pity, because as a result the treatments had no effect. Nobody saw that I quickly became overstimulated. I remember participating in a cycling event with the day care patients. We rode 30 kilometres on our bicycles in the summer heat. When I came home, I had a fit of anger out of the blue and smashed a coffee table. I scared myself stiff. I was totally overstimulated by all this intense exercise, the bustle and the heat, but didn't know it then.'* A family member was diagnosed with PDD-NOS. This jumpstarted Karin into reading more about autism. She recognised many of the symptoms and mentioned this to her then practitioner. *'It was impossible for me to be autistic, I was told. I had a few characteristics at most. Nothing more. As she was the expert, I relied on her judgment. So it couldn't be that I had autism.'*

Exactly this kind of judgment causes a large group of people with autism not to be recognised and acknowledged. They have not been diagnosed. Karin explains: *'You then continue wrestling with fits of anger, crying fits, panic and lack of overview. Things don't work out. You keep losing your job. Relationships don't flourish.'* A lot of these people end up having to deal with social services, where no one knows a thing about autism. *'In the education system, teachers are trained to recognise autism in children. It should be the same in social services,'* says Karin. *'The prevailing image of autism mainly deals with children and hardly touches on adults. If they are recognised as being autistic in the first place, they are children who haven't grown out of it. And if an adult has adapted his behaviour, the autism diagnosis doesn't exist any more. A person like that doesn't fit the perception of autism. But inside, this adult has not changed at all. He has only found a way of soldiering on. He would actually need an adjusted position at work to do full justice to his talents. But that's not possible. His autism isn't recognised, so there's no diagnosis.'*

If the 'autism' diagnosis has actually been made, there are other problems. *'If someone has ASD, people often focus on the situation at home. Only if someone functions well at home, is this person deemed to be able to work. Or so the prevailing opinion reads. But in my case, you can wait until the cows come home before I could do the housekeeping by myself. That moment will not come. Of course it is important to ensure balance and support at home. But don't expect a person with autism to put all his energy into it, as that is usually not where his talents lie. That's also why it's important to consider work or daytime activities carefully. What is the person able to do, and what isn't he? What does he like doing? What is he good at?'*

Karin is happy with her employer. He offers her the opportunity to develop and express her talents. The work is an enrichment for Karin and provides structure in her life. It is therefore not surprising that Karin now ventures to call herself a successful autistic. *'I've conquered many problems. I've learned to live with others by organising things in such a way that they bother me the least. I've arranged my assistance optimally. I can use my talents. I haven't yet fully developed myself, by a long shot. I want to examine, for example, the symptoms that adults with autism have. Stimuli-processing problems in particular. In addition, I want to carry on with drawing up a questionnaire for adults on sensory functioning. This already exists for children. Because if you know how the senses have developed, you can understand the processing of sensory stimuli. In people with autism, this processing of stimuli often varies a lot. If we have an insight into this, we know what support we have to deploy in the workplace.'* Karin mentions the example of a client who had problems with eating. Her sense of taste was constantly changing. On one occasion, a jam sandwich was tasty, the next time it wasn't. As a practical solution Karin suggested spreading jam on just a corner of the sandwich first, to check on how it tasted at that moment. *'You might say this woman was hoaxed by her senses.'*

We ask Karin what she thinks are the qualities of people with ASD. Resolutely she replies: *'People with autism may have considerable talents, but no two persons with autism are the same. Some can work very accurately. Take the example of a layout assistant in a printing company. That type of work involves dealing with tenths of millimetres. Someone like that doesn't need to perform at speed, but will have to deliver quality. He is in the right place. But there are also people with autism who are unable to do this. They can easily miss the mark by half a centimetre and it doesn't bother them. Both have the will and drive for precision, but for one person this leads to different result than it does for the other. Sometimes you can be very good at something, but that doesn't necessarily mean that you enjoy it. And the other way around. You are not always good at the things you like doing. This also applies to people without autism, by the way. If you don't have autism, there are more possibilities open to you. You have more choice. Unfortunately, many people with autism don't work. A pity, as it is important for their talents to be seen. People with autism are still too easily seen as the "Rainman", as a retarded person. It's this image, among other things, that causes people with autism to have fewer opportunities in the job market, whereas they certainly have qualities that can add value to a company. If we focus on their qualities and provide sufficient support, a person with autism gets the chance to develop and be valuable for the employer and society. He also feels better, as it feels great to be good at something and mean something for the company, after all.'*

The fact that people with autism also have talents doesn't mean that autism can be regarded as a quality, is Karin's firm belief. *'For many, autism is agony. We do get there, but it is hard. I prefer to speak of the power of autism, with self-insight being important. There are people with autism for whom auto-reflection is very difficult. Consequently, they are quick to blame others when they get into trouble. For that reason they are difficult to coach. But many people with ASD blame themselves when something goes wrong. And because that happens frequently, they think they are worthless. They often feel stupid and clumsy, while in most cases there is nothing the matter with their intelligence. For them it's important to realise that their problems are rooted in their disabilities, and not in their person. These people need self-confidence. That is a long road.'* Nicely put. We realise that we cannot talk about the quality of autism just like that.

'What we require to be able to turn out well,' Karin concludes, *'is self-reflection. Thinking about ourselves, seeing consequences, being open to advice, being able to communicate to a certain extent, willingness to learn and to change within the boundaries of our possibilities. Even when we are sometimes only able to take baby steps. That's no deal breaker. A certain amount of courage is also required. If you keep on developing your strong points, the contrast with your limitations continually grows, as these do not change. That may be confrontational sometimes. It's therefore important to accept your limitations and accept help. We are, in fact, in a wheelchair. The difficulty with that wheelchair is that others cannot see it. It's an invisible wheelchair. We often have to explain that we need that wheelchair, that we require assistance and adaptations to be able to*

function. The quintessential thing is to accept that we have to live in this wheelchair. That we have the courage to be both vulnerable and strong, and that we maintain our self-respect. That is my guiding principle.'

14.

'LET'S OPEN OUR EYES'

Dirk Rombaut, writer of the original business plan for, start-up coordinator of, and now sales manager within Passwerk, a Belgian secondment agency whose employees (test engineers) all have ASD.

' *We started in March 2008 with four test engineers. At the beginning of 2011, we are already 32. It's our ambition to deploy some 100 test engineers in the long term. But honestly, it doesn't matter how many, even if there are only 40 next year. It's the goal that matters,* ' Dirk Rombaut says. Passwerk is a company that tests software functionality and performance. All test engineers working at Passwerk are people of normal to high ability with ASD. Precisely because they have ASD, and because they are coached by professionals from Passwerk, they are extremely well suited for this work. How did Dirk become involved in a world he hardly knew existed before? And how did he manage to turn Passwerk into such a success?

Dirk Rombaut has 20 years in personnel management behind him. His last job before he started at Passwerk was as Human Resources Director Benelux at Royal and Sun Alliance. He then started working as a consultant at the VDAB (Vlaamse Dienst voor Arbeidsbemiddeing en Beroepsopleiding) a Flemish Employment and Training Agency. In view of his business and project experience he was asked, in August 2007, to start up a new business for people with ASD. The initiative for founding this unique company was born a year earlier, when Willy Piedfort of the De Ploeg consultation centre, which helps people with an employment disability find a job, and Kristiene Reyniers of the

Ergasia employment initiative for people with ASD, together attended a conference on ASD in Poland. On their return, Willy and Kristiene decided to form a steering group with the goal of founding a company that offered individuals, with a normal IQ, who had ASD, an IT job in the normal market. *'My then boss at the VDAB was also asked to participate in the steering group. As it turned out to be difficult to realise the plan, they asked me if I wanted to implement the idea. Actually, I wasn't enthusiastic at all. What did I know about autism? Furthermore, I had never before founded a business, and was not omniscient as far as IT was concerned. I nevertheless considered it a fascinating challenge and set to work on it, but did so in a businesslike manner, following all the steps, from the project definition report to the business plan. And I wanted to learn more about autism and IT. To carry out research and talk to lots of people.'*

Dirk became fascinated and enthused. *'I realised increasingly that for people with ASD, it is a lot more difficult to make themselves seem in society. At the same time, they have extraordinary abilities which are not used. As my research progressed, more and more I considered Willy and Kristiene's idea to be a social model. That was exactly why so much appealed to me, and I really wanted to take it further.'* Dirk drafted his business plan and contacted the director of the Copenhagen-based company Specialisterne, Thorkil Sonne. At the said conference in Poland, this Danish company presented a success story. Following this contact, Dirk was forced to conclude that, unfortunately, the Danish plan was by definition unsuitable for Flanders. *'Each country has its own social situation. Furthermore, Thorkil's point of view differs from ours. He has an autistic son and therefore approached the matter with "gut feeling". He said that his son's abilities were not recognised by society. That is why, in the first instance, Thorkil distanced himself from academics and assistance workers, professional people with the know-how for coaching people with ASD. We eventually chose a Flemish approach with locally embedded people and professionals.'*

Although Dirk knows that people with ASD have limitations, he initially focuses only on their capabilities. *'If you include their limitations in the thought process too soon, it has a limiting effect.'* We ask Dirk what he regards as positive qualities in people with ASD. *'People with autism often have strong analytical skills, an eye for detail and a sense of order. Some of them have expert skills, such as a strong visual memory. They are enthusiastic workers who are reliable and keep their agreements. And they are consistent in their behaviour, have no hidden agendas, and they are honest and loyal. Having few social interests can be an advantage, as no time is wasted on maintaining social interactions during work time. People with ASD are in fact able to do things that others are not good at or do not want to do in the longer term.'* As Dirk did not want to found just another business, but a company with a clear profile, he focused on software testing. *'The position of test engineer as we now know it, did not exist back then. Test engineers were people who focused on test design and test coordination. The latter requires a lot of communication and is therefore difficult for people with ASD. Therefore, I proposed to focus Passwerk on just the executive part. This had a number of consequences. We had to focus on big and specialised companies and leave a clear job profile. What would and what wouldn't fit this profile?'*

The idea was starting to become a reality. But then the 'money' problem raised its head. *'That was not easy. Everybody standing on the sidelines said: "Go for it! It is a great initiative!" Until demands were made on their wallets. They didn't believe that Passwerk could actually be a success.'* Eventually Passwerk becomes a reality after all. Two parties from the IT sector joined: Ordina Belgium and M2Q (Cronos Group). *'In addition, a number of organisations active in dealing with the issue of ASD put in symbolic amounts. I think it is important for the company to be embedded, both in the normal economic world and in the world of ASD. The government provides grants on certain conditions. A few members of the Flanders Business Angels Netwerk (BAN) have also joined in.'* BAN is a platform with added value where starting or expanding entrepreneurs looking for high-risk capital are brought into contact with informal, private investors, the so-called Business Angels. These Business Angels bring in not only money, but also their own know-how, experience and contacts.

And then the moment arrived. In February 2008 Passwerk came into existence as a cooperative society with limited liability with a social objective under Belgian law. The primary aim of Passwerk is to let people with ASD work in a normal business environment, guided by a coach. But how do you reach the market? Making contacts directly proved to be difficult. That's why Passwerk decided to work via a distribution system. The distributors are Ordina Belgium and M2Q (Cronos Group). They introduced Passwerk to the market. *'That has a number of big advantages, as the market sets demands that Passwerk cannot meet by itself. For example, in the framework of the Public Contracts Act. Large suppliers work with a Request for Information (RFI), Request for Proposal (RFP) and a Request for Quotation (RFQ), framework contracts or framework agreements. Passwerk was initially unable to offer all these. Furthermore, the distributors have considerable experience with software testing.'* If a position becomes vacant with a client, a discussion between the client, Dirk and a technically trained person from the distributors takes place. *'Only if we are 99 per cent sure to be technically successful in a company, do we take the next step: carrying out a site survey. This is done by our job coaches. The site survey relates to both the physical environment and the corporate culture in which our test engineers end up. That way, we are able to make the ideal match between the demand/work environment for the client's and our test engineers. If we actually have a suitable candidate, we take the plunge. Otherwise, we let the assignment pass. We want to avoid the situation where our employee becomes frustrated by the working conditions, which would result in the client not being happy.'*

The preparations had been made and the structure had been implemented. Now, only the people were missing, but this challenge turned out to not be so difficult to overcome. It wasn't even necessary to advertise. The candidates streamed in via the Belgian non-profit organisations actively dealing with the autism spectrum, from GPs, coaches of autistics, schools and other organisations.

After Passwerk has analysed the profile of a new applicant, an induction follows, which is guided by a job coach (psychologist, remedial teacher or social worker with knowledge of ASD). The candidate hears what is expected of him, about the environment where he will be placed, what the training entails, etc. *'And the job coach judges whether the candidate can move around independently, can master the English language sufficiently, and perform adequately in a normal business environment.'*

Perform in a normal business environment? Is that possible? Working in an open-plan office, for example, is not optimal for people with ASD. Dirk smiles and says: *'We often reproach people with autism for not being very flexible. But people without autism are good at it as well. My experience? In the initial phase, you shouldn't go to an employer saying "remember this, don't forget that". That's too complex for them. But once the employee is in his place, a lot is possible and you can create the actual conditions required for people with ASD.'* Before the Passwerk test engineer sits at his actual desk, he engages in an entrance process. This consists of the following steps: induction, specific testing to determine the mental abilities and certain competencies, follow-up discussion of test results, a three-week assessment procedure and an evaluation assessment with advisory discussion. And then the candidate becomes a Passwerk employee. An average of 20 per cent of the candidates (with a ratio of 1 woman to 3 men) successfully completes the selection procedure. These employees then receive a one-month training within Passwerk – taught by the distributors – to become test engineers. On completion, the Passwerk employees are presented with an international software testing certificate (ISTQB). And only then do they finally get placed with the client. On average, the Passwerk workers have a 30–32-hour working week. *'The client is, of course, also prepared for the arrival of the employee, by way of a presentation on ASD. Our job coach accompanies the test engineer on his first working day and stays there for as long as necessary.'*

Apart from the entrance procedure, intensive coaching and follow-up of the employees is crucial to the success of Passwerk. This is done in the first instance by the job coach. This coach is always, every day, available to the test engineer and can be contacted both by telephone and by email. He or she is the point of contact regarding both the living and the work environment of the test engineer. *'Sometimes, simply the arrival of a new coffee machine may cause stress,'* Dirk says. The job coach also visits the client every week to evaluate and optimise the collaboration. *'Consider the following example. The test engineer's boss literally gives him a pat on the shoulder. Well intentioned. But this test engineer cannot stand physical touch at all, and quits within 30 minutes. These, therefore, are issues that the job coach also discusses with the client.'*

Passwerk thinks it is important to emphasise the positive qualities of people with ASD in all kinds of ways. The company was created by focusing first and foremost on these positive characteristics. Passwerk hopes that this approach will lead to less stigmatising and a better, more valuable social integration of people with ASD. Over the past few years, a first few steps have been carefully and tactfully taken. The concept works. Passwerk is making a business profit. But that is not the main thing. Companies are satisfied with the Passwerk employees, who are extremely accurate and dedicated. *'People who are not autistic, often don't want a job as a test engineer. The work is too monotonous. The consequence is a shortage of a test engineers. Companies then tend to hire people with a less suitable profile, but that is not necessary at all. Look at our Passwerk employees. But above all, Passwerk is especially advantageous for the employees themselves. They return to a social network and work on their independence. They get appreciation and are once more part of something.'*

Passwerk is solid. But, as is the case with many initiatives, at first it was mainly *'out of the box thinking'*, as Dirk calls it. *'If I said I needed three weeks for assessment, I was told: "Dirk, you have no idea of the costs involved! Just cancel it. It won't work anyway." But I stayed the course. I believed in it. Now these same people say: "Of course, that's what we need." And that's the way many things went in the initial phase. Can we cut back on our job coaches? No, definitely not! This framework is what makes our approach a success. Passwerk is and continues to be built on the custom-made approach.'*

Before starting at Passwerk, Dirk knew nothing about autism. But now he has 'got the bug', he says. *'Autism continues to fascinate me.'* As we can see when we want to round off the discussion and leave Antwerp. Dirk thinks, then continues: *'It is neurotypical to pigeon-hole things. This social method helps us structure reality and is very successful. But it also creates victims. We have excluded people for years and now we talk about including them. In other words, first we threw them all out and now we want to bring them back again. Something went really wrong. And before you know it, bringing them back will go wrong as well. Inclusion needs to be done with the necessary care. But do we really get the opportunity to do so? We need to look far beyond just "return on investment". This concerns the entire picture. When we do, there will be many more possibilities, of all sorts, to make use of people's potential. From a social point of view, we will all benefit from that. I see how the dedication of our Passwerk employees inspires companies. They respond with words like: "We can learn from their drive". But no, we have ended up in a market society where we look for the impossible. It doesn't exist. We constantly frustrate employees by saying: "That is your responsibility. It is part of your job." After some time, these people are so pressured that it makes them ill. So, let's open our eyes and see the value of people with ASD so that they can reclaim their rightful place in society.'*

THE OPINION OF PASSWERK EMPLOYEES

Sam: *This is the first time that I have worked for more than a year for one and the same employer. It's also the first time I haven't yet gone to work unwillingly for a single day. The coaching gives me so much breathing space. I can and am allowed to talk about the things that bother me. If there are problems, they are not just swept under the carpet.*

Dirk: *The work environment will be adapted to your way of working and not the other way around. When I read this about Passwerk, I had found my place. In the past, people did not always realise that there already are people who are well suited to working behind the scenes in customer service, to give but one example. A soft skill, such as being easy-going, is for most people no big deal. However, for me it is the biggest stumbling block.*

Johan: *After a long search and lots of training and doing less interesting jobs, thanks to Passwerk I have finally found something I like doing and that gives me satisfaction. So I can safely say that Passwerk has helped put me back on my feet and has offered me a new future.*

THE OPINION OF EMPLOYERS

Erik Jennen, project manager at Ordina Belgium: *Developers usually don't like systematic testing work, but people with ASD do. Thanks to the perfectionism of the people at Passwerk, we can count on high quality in the development results.*

Marijke Verhavert, section manager of the Department of Administration (Flemish Government): *I especially notice that the quality of the products has improved and that attention to the testing cycle has increased. Tests are simply much more efficient and that makes our customers happy as well.*

Jan Hammenecker, director of corporate systems and communication for the Flemish Society for Water Supply: *The software package for the invoice of the water supply is complex and the programme logic is relatively difficult. However, the Passwerk testers adapted to the work extremely quickly; during the training for working with the package, one of them straightaway even discovered a mistake in the complex invoicing module.*

15.

'SOCIETY IS READY FOR IT'

Marcel Hurkens, psychologist and founder of NOXQS. The letters stand for 'No Excuses'.

There are a few companies in the Netherlands that have made a very conscious decision to work with people with autism because of their qualities. Specialisterren in Utrecht is one such company, consisting of 12 men with ASD, testing software for various companies such as RTL Television, Ditzo Insurances and Wegener Publishers. A big difference, compared with Passwerk (see Chapter 14) is that its employees are not being outsourced. They work in a screened-off environment at the Specialisterren premises. AutiTalent in Nieuwegein, the Netherlands, does outsource. AutiTalent's services consist of clearing up and digitalising archives. We visit yet another company, NOXQS, and speak to its founder and director, Marcel Hurkens.

The office of NOXQS is located above the Dream Restaurant and Conference Centre, where people with and without a limitation join forces to provide perfect service. We are greeted by the smell of freshly baked apple pie when we come in. Many laughing and friendly faces. If you've got out of bed on the wrong side, your mood will change for the better here. We are a little early and first have a cup of coffee.

Once upstairs, we make for the conference room together with Marcel. On our way we pass what Marcel refers to as 'the bar'. It is a heightened table with 'bar stools'. A large computer screen hangs on the short end. A few NOXQS employees are talking to each other and regularly looking at the screen, which shows a prototype of a NOXQS product. We shake hands with them. We will talk to two of them about their work later on (see text box at the end of the chapter).

A little more than seven years ago, Marcel was working as a psychologist, working with people with disabilities. Together with colleague Jeroen van Schaik, he started up NOXQS in 2004. Marcel: *'We thought of new improvements in caring for people with disabilities. Things like simplifying information for people with learning disabilities, such as care plans, information leaflets and brochures, especially by using lots of graphic information. It is about visualisation. After a while, multimedia became an increasingly important tool for us. The fact is that people with an intellectual disability can be better informed with image and sound than by means of text. To provide an example, we make voters' guides based on visual information for people with a disability. That is interesting not only for people with an intellectual disability, but also for people with poor literacy skills or none at all. At some point, we made a computer interface for someone with a severe intellectual disability. This computer allows this person to do things he couldn't do otherwise. For example, something as simple as listening to his own choice of music. That man can't speak. Thanks to photos on the computer he is now able to communicate with his environment. A number of care institutions are using a comparable interface developed by us. At the time, we mainly outsourced the production of the software for these types of products. In January 2010 we met two boys with autism at the day centre for people with an intellectual disability. However, they did not have an intellectual disability. We thought: this is ridiculous! They both had a passion for IT. We contacted the day centre (as they were under treatment there) and the unemployment agency, to discuss whether we could receive wage cost subsidy so that they could come and work for us. The day centre and the unemployment agency next asked us if we couldn't offer a workplace for more people with autism. A U-turn for our organisation, as it would then become a business unit in itself.'*

The U-turn was made. And that is how, in January 2011, a new business unit was created: NOXQS Labs. It employed ten young people on disability benefits who had autism, an above-average IQ and a passion for IT – which was the selection criteria. *'They are talented lads. The trick is to ensure that they start using their talents. We want to provide them with the right environment to do so. We coach them for a three-year period, and by then they should have the capabilities and the freedom to go work elsewhere. They can also stay if they want to, but we don't want to create a culture that makes it impossible for them to leave.'* No pampering, then. *'By the end of those three years we also want them to be certified as a programmer, or at least to have mastered a number of computer languages. On the one hand we do the things they are interested in, but on the other, we are, after all, a company that needs to earn money. We have to find a middle ground here. A lot of work is generated by the other business unit, NOXQS. We're working on building a platform that is equipped with applications. A lot of the lads can work on that. They also build games for children with an intellectual disability and perform web design for other companies and organisations.'*

During this first year Marcel still receives wage cost subsidy, but later on things will become less secure. Wage costs will see a steep rise. The young people are supported by people from within the company itself, people who complement each other well. *'One is knowledgeable about programming and the other is very good at ordering. They can work well with people with autism. One of them was even recently diagnosed with autism himself. He really recognises a lot of things,'* Marcel says. It is interesting to note that the boys also collaborate a lot. *'The image of people with autism who can only work with earplugs and blinkers is wrong. They collaborate excellently, as long as the goal of the collaboration is clear. They discuss a problem with each other, and need to have an interest in getting it solved, otherwise they can't proceed. They depend on each other for that. Only when the collaboration involves all types of vague processes do things become difficult.'* One of the job coaches at first worked on the workfloor, with the boys. After some time, however, they decided that he had to leave. They became too dependent on him. *'Everybody was asking him for help the whole time. Which of course wasn't exactly the idea.'*

With one exception they all work four days per week, for around eight hours per day. All the boys come under some form of assist living arrangement. Marcel himself does not want to become some sort of assistance worker. He notices that the boys like having this division between assistance and work. *'Some of them sometimes entice us into playing the assistance worker role. A form of acquired helplessness. They think, I only have to snap my fingers and there is another assistance worker. We don't respond to that. We emphasise that we either have to earn money here or we'll have to close shop. When we explain, they understand.'* Being production-oriented sometimes does pose a problem. According to Marcel, not everybody fully realises this. *'There are boys who don't always make the distinction between gaming at home and being at work here. We need to show some flexibility in that regard.'* Marcel explains that people without autism can't imagine what it is like to be autistic. *'Some of them are already dog-tired the moment they arrive here in the morning. When they are late you don't say: "One more time and it's goodbye." They are not average employees. And the main thing, after all, is that the work they produce is sufficient for us to pay them, one way or another. We are considering, next year, letting them be free one day per week to do their own work. On that day they won't have to work on an assignment and can work on what they like and find interesting. I do want them to make a presentation then. And of course, they need to do something that is useful for the company.'*

The boys with autism who work at NOXQS don't yet visit customers; they work in the office above the Dream Conference Centre. Marcel expects, however, that it will happen at some point. *'After all, you can't keep them in the same office for three years and then expect them to be able to spread their wings and move to another company,'* he says. The bar needs to be set ever higher in the course of these three years. Their world needs to expand at some point. Marcel doesn't approve of overly standardising the tasks his employees have to do. He thinks that then the creativity of people with autism would not be used to it's full advantage. *'They think differently than you and I, and consequently can conceive very different ideas. If you only let them test software, it boils down to people without autism thinking up the product and the people with autism being relegated merely to seeing if it works. I, on the contrary, notice a talent for creative work, allowing them to be more lucrative, which could enhance their value to the organisation. If I were to have a number of the people who work here just test software, they would go crazy. They cannot manage that.'*

What is important to Marcel is that talents don't lie fallow. *'It's a terrible waste if their talents are unused. Furthermore, it contributes to their personal happiness. If you do things that make you feel good, others profit most from that as well, as a company and as a society.'*

If the concept works, nothing will keep NOXQS from implementing it in other places in the Netherlands. *'Let's first ensure it is going to work here,'* Marcel says, putting things into perspective. *'We are not successful yet and we still need to invent and experience many things. We are, however, looking hard for a way for these young people to be successful, and if it doesn't work here, we have to find another way. Society is ready for it. After all, you can see more and more, at the unemployment agency as well, that anyone using his or her talents becomes important. Certainly now, in the time of cutbacks. The flip side of the welfare state is insufficient stimulus for people to use their talents.'* That sounds logical, but this initiative is special. Shouldn't the ideal scenario be that other employers who – unlike Marcel – don't have a care worker background, need to offer people with autism more chances? Marcel sees that things are changing slowly but surely. *'Regulations are adapted, making it more interesting for employers to hire people with a disability. The Slotervaart hospital in Amsterdam, for example, is hiring 100 people on disability benefits. By means of job carving, or the creation of new positions by clustering tasks, they have made positions suitable for people with a disability. There is an element of idealism involved, but the Slotervaart hospital really isn't going to spend money just to get people off of benefits. There has to be a return on investment.'*

THE OPINION OF NOXQS LABS EMPLOYEES

Ezra Teunissen and Joeri Kerkhof both work at NOXQS Labs; they are trainee programmers. Both have ASD. They collaborate on a virtual interpretation of a website without text. They are actually building a virtual environment where people can walk in, meet and look at informative short films. *'It is for a target group that needs something more visual than just text,'* Ezra says. *'The access to this virtual world will also be made very easy,'* Joeri adds. *'You shouldn't make people who are going to use it first have to go through an entire set-up procedure. They can't do that. The intention is that these people learn things in a simple and playful manner. But they shouldn't get the idea that they are learning something. If they do, they won't feel like it.'*

Joeri and Ezra belong to the ten trainee programmers with a disability who are now on a three-year job-training programme at NOXQS. Ezra did voluntary work before joining NOXQS. He programmed games for a foundation that supports adults with a disability and children with developmental delay, and supported them at school and with their living, working and day activities. Before that he participated in day activities at a Dutch centre specialising in autism. For some time, Joeri earned money building websites and creating applications, for instance for the iPad and the iPhone. He worked from home. Joeri and Ezra did the NOXQS IT training together, so they have known each other for some time. Incidentally, both were in special education. Joeri: *'Luckily, our school had a games room where I could enjoy myself, but for the rest I hated school. Except for IT, I haven't passed a single subject.'*

At NOXQS, on the other hand, they feel really at home. Ezra: *'It is working and learning all in one, which really appeals to me. There is a lot of independent study involved, but you can ask your colleagues for help if you can't work it out. That's an important goal of the company: working things out together. We share our passion for IT, and that's why this collaboration works well. The people working here are also very nice.'* Joeri: *'A big difference from school is that you do assignments at school and nothing happens with it. Here, you make something the customer can use. That is useful.'* They clearly value the appreciation they get for their work and hope that the NOXQS Labs initiative will be successful. But they are somewhat concerned. Joeri: *'I think it will be difficult, and that there are going to be changes. There may be too few assignments later on, or too little money to keep going.* Ezra: *'We've only just begun and still have a lot to learn. We're working on professionalisation and this process is getting better all the time.'*

16.

'WE WANT TO BE OURSELVES!'

Carlo Post (53), founder of *Autisme Ten Top* ('Autism at the Top'), the Dutch network for and around highly educated people with ASD. Carlo works at ASK Community Systems as senior developer. He has Asperger's.

'At the end of 2007 I launched the idea of Autisme Ten Top, *the goal of which is a broader acceptance of autism. People with ASD are allowed to be who they really are.'* When we visit him at home in Utrecht (the Netherlands), Carlo has a clear message. Outside it is freezing, we listen to his story over a cup of coffee and an almond pastry. After years of wrestling sadness, frustration and disempowerment, now he can really be himself. Now at last he is successful, both in his work and as a human being. *' I have a good job and a nice family with my wife and two teenagers.'*

Carlo Post found out only five years ago that he had ASD. At last everything began to fall into place for him. But up until then...he had spent almost half a lifetime pioneering, that's what it comes down to. Care professionals and employers didn't understand him, and he didn't understand them. *'I had depressions but couldn't explain them. I advanced by trial and error.'*

Carlo Post graduated in mathematics. Only just. He has difficulty with planning. Consequently, he wasn't always able to finish assignments in time. He was also too much of a perfectionist. But he wanted to go on. Applying for a job was the next step. *'But I hadn't learned how to do that. I just continued applying without landing a job, and eventually things went really wrong. I ended up in a vicious circle and feeling frustrated. I was completely stressed out.'* Carlo was admitted to a psychiatric ward of a general hospital. But after a short while 'the bird' was ready to stretch his wings again. *'If you cannot help me within a week, I'll leave,'* he told the support workers. It soon became evident that they couldn't help him. *'I am unusual as far as communication is concerned. They didn't do anything about that. In addition, I am a practising Catholic, to which they couldn't relate. That was the last straw for me.'* Carlo had had enough, and literally walked away. He packed his bags in front of a therapy group. But what next? Carlo read books, looking for information and help. He wanted to know what was wrong with him. At that time he didn't yet know that his problems had everything to do with autism. He was 28-years-old, full of questions and unemployed. At his own initiative and expense – *'I had to pay for everything myself'* – Carlo turned to a psychologist. A good choice, because for the first time in his life he had the feeling that someone understood him and took him seriously. In addition, the psychologist, a Protestant, was accepting of Carlo and his faith – something that made him feel good, as faith is something to hold on to for Carlo. The psychologist helped him pursue his path. He was finally able to take up where he had left off after finishing his studies.

The municipal social service department at the time exempted him from the obligation to apply for jobs. He doesn't need to work, but it is not in his nature to be idle. Carlo plunged into voluntary work for the 'People Looking for Work' project helping people find a job, in a particular neighbourhood in Utrecht. His tasks involved taking care of publicity and planning the courses taught within the framework of this project. After retraining to become a programmer, Carlo succeeded in getting a job at Comsys International, a company focused on telecommunication applications. Right up his street.

He finally had a 'real' job and was happy. The start of a new period in his life. *'I have programmed and built applications for ten years for this company. At some point, management noticed that I was good at analysing. When there were major software malfunctions, they called me in. They saw I could solve the problems quickly and neatly. I was then asked to do technical maintenance of the software. I agreed and have been doing this work for about five years.'*

Carlo seemed to have found his place. He felt at ease, his supervisor understood him and let him do the things he is good at. But then things changed. The company went belly-up. Fortunately, he could stay on for the relaunch, but his luck was short-lived. His father suddenly passed away. *'He died all of a sudden of a cerebral infarction during a bicycle ride. He worked at Eindhoven University of Technology.'* The passing of his father affected Carlo to such an extent that he suffered burnout and reported sick. Again, he was hit by a period of uncertainty and needed to gather all his strength and courage to rise from the malaise. Again he succeeded, after some time. He wanted to resume work, but then encountered unexpected problems. After the relaunch of the company, the management had been replaced. Unlike his previous supervisor, the new one had no understanding for Carlo. *'He went to great lengths to get me out. I had to go for economic reasons. In reality he didn't know how to handle me. I saw and felt it. I'm good at analysing what is behind the communication. So, so…so, yes…'* Carlo sighs audibly and stares pensively ahead of him. It hurts to be reminded of this period. *'I was very nearly 46 and I was at home. I had been eliminated.'*

Carlo wanted to get back work, but was forced to live on sickness benefits. He still wasn't required to apply for jobs. But Carlo didn't throw in the towel this time either. He took the time to get things clear for himself and once again sought counselling. At the same time, he trained himself to build websites, working on the website for the parish of certain neighbourhoods in Utrecht. And then, at last, after all those years, the truth came out. Carlo had Asperger's, or so the official diagnosis went. *'As a child, I had actually been diagnosed with an autism-related disorder. Classic autism was not possible as I would also have had to have learning difficulties. That was thinking at the time. ASD as such was unknown back then.'* The Asperger's diagnosis was a shock for Carlo, but at the same time the pieces of the jigsaw fell into place. A great sense of relief followed.

In 2006 Carlo started the Individual Re-integration Agreement course under supervision of Jacques van Hees, a personal coach with his own agency. People who cannot find a job straightaway, and who have been on unemployment benefit for at least six months, or receive a partial benefit under the Dutch Disablement Insurance Act or Disablement Assistance (Young Persons) Act, have been able to take advantage of this course since 1 January 2004. Carlo chose the rehabilitation agency himself. An agency that suited him. The agency explained step-by-step how he could succeed in finding a job. Carlo regained his self-confidence. *'We decided from then on that I would indicate at every job interview that I have Asperger's, and what that means for me and the employer. I wanted to clearly explain my positive and negative points. The reactions I subsequently got from potential employers were positive. They appreciated my honesty. I am glad that I took this step.'*

When we ask him what his strong and weak points actually are, Carlo answers: *'I have good analytical skills. I know how structures and programming environments are set up. I see the links right away. My memory is excellent as well, as is my ready knowledge. I can do a satisfactory job of explaining.'* With pride, Carlo says casually that in the past he obtained a teaching qualification. We look at him in astonishment. Don't people with autism often have difficulties with interpersonal communication? *'That is right. But there are various types of communication skills. You shouldn't let someone with autism try to convince anyone or sell anything. But counselling people, knowing what goes on with them, that is what we are good at. I know many people with ASD who are career consultants. They achieve good results with people with ASD. They know the problems from personal experience.'* OK, so a qualification to teach. We ask him if he has more surprises up his sleeve for us. He laughs and continues to talk about the skills he has and the ones he hasn't. *'Things have improved the last few years, but I continue to find reading non-verbal signs difficult. I don't always succeed. If people ask too much of me, I will also be difficult.'* So far, we haven't noticed this much during the interview. It is important to Carlo that he can and must concentrate. He tells us that in his current job he sits in the far corner of the open-plan office. A quiet place. *'I can work while listening to classical music on my earphones. That is better for me.'*

So Carlo had a new job as Senior Developer at ASK Community Systems. *'I already had my eye on this company in 2006. I saw a vacancy in the newspaper. I applied but was rejected at first because my portfolio contained too little web technology. Before I got this job, I did independent study on this subject. Now, this parish in Utrecht is on the map of the World Wide Web.'* Totally unexpectedly, Carlo received a telephone call from ASK. They had a vacancy for a programmer. That was more up Carlo's street. *'I had a really nice conversation with my supervisor and the technical chief at the time. After a second meeting I was given an annual contract. Incredibly, I was then offered a steady job — at the age of 48. I feel great in this company.'*

In 2005, Carlo was diagnosed with Asperger's, as he had already told us. Shortly after being diagnosed he decided to join PAS Netherlands (see textbox on p.80). Carlo has dedicated himself to this club, especially where it involves walking tours. He is an enthusiastic hiker. He does night walks of 50 to 60 kilometres with his son. *'At PAS I have organised 15 walks for the General Federation of Hikers on the Autism Spectrum.'*

At the end of 2007 Carlo pitched his *Autisme Ten Top* idea. *'For autistics who are highly educated, next to nothing is done. Society has certain expectations of highly educated people. We, people with ASD, cannot meet them. We are not good at communication skills. That's the crux. Our hands are tied. We continuously feel we have to present ourselves differently to squeeze into the straightjacket of the (socially) average person. That is very stressful and frustrating. These attempts, furthermore, lead to unnatural behaviour, which only increases the risk of rejection. The problem is that a large number of employers have little knowledge and understanding regarding autism, just like many career counsellors and other support workers. That is why it is so important for people both with and without autism to talk to each other, and especially to learn from each other.'*

In 2008 Carlo, together with Jaap Brand (see Chapter 1), decided to take the plunge and *Autisme Ten Top* became established on LinkedIn, one of the many social media outlets. The group now has more than 500 members, consisting of care providers and people with ASD. Information is exchanged back and forth. There are a lot of discussions. It works; the response is massive. Carlo is happy. *'I didn't dare hope for this.'*

However, Carlo wants the discussion to be not only digital, but also personal. When necessary, he takes to the road. *'If an employer asks me to talk about autism, I will. Spreading the message, in whatever manner, is important. Employers need to realise that autism works on the workfloor. Every organisation needs a number of people that stand out if you want to implement innovation. There lies the power of the autistic person. It is very detrimental that autistics are faced with prejudice, being compared with the "Rainman", the stereotype of an autistic man. Or take the image of the autistic as a "nerd" or computer expert who is good with computers, but not with human interaction. I am of the opinion that every company needs an autistic employee. An autistic person can, for example, infallibly bring unspoken communication to light. We've already talked about that. I experienced it myself at the time when I was dismissed. I knew that the director wanted to push me out. He found out to his cost. I called in the union.'*

The obsessions autistic persons so often have may be useful to a company, too. That sounds strange. *'I have, for example, an obsession with dates. Tell me your dates of birth for example. I know exactly on what day you were born.'* We put it to the test and state our dates of birth: 12 October 1963 and 8 October 1962. *'A Saturday and a Monday,'* Carlo says after only a second. Amazing, but what use is this knowledge to an employer? Carlo gives an example. *'At work, we had a problem with a planning board. In weeks 14 and 43, on the Sunday, it posed problems. As I am good at dates, I knew that week 14 is usually at the end of March and week 43 at the end of October. I saw it at once. The planning board didn't take daylight savings properly into account.'* While other programmers would probably need days to solve this apparently simple problem, Carlo was able to help his employer right away. That saves a lot of time, energy, and therefore money. Employers often see only the negative side of an employee with ASD, but an obsession with dates can indeed be turned to good account. Employers also often forget that autistics have an extraordinarily good memory. A characteristic that can certainly be used in an organisation, as Carlo has experienced. *'With my previous employer, I was secretary to the works council. As my memory is so good, I could infallibly retrieve certain meeting documents. I am a walking archive, as it were, and they have often used it.'*

Carlo finally feels good. Not only at work, but also on a personal level. He knows that he has Asperger's, and has made something out of it, both for himself and for others. He doesn't regard autism as a handicap. Of course, he finds certain things hard, such as interpersonal communication, as already mentioned. *'My wife is better at communicating with our children. On the other hand, I do go with my daughter to the theatre. I spend hours behind the computer with my son, who is also very good at programming. We make all kinds of web applications and movies. Movies that you can move from YouTube to play lists.'* For Carlo and his son, a knack; for us, a large question mark. We see once again that every human being is unique. Everybody has his good and bad sides, his knowledge, skills and experience. Autistic or otherwise.

The guinea pigs in their cage by the window have fallen silent during their carer's story — as have we. A look into Carlo's world is something special and makes us realise that we can still learn a lot about autism. It has been a fight for Carlo, a battle of more than 45 years. Only since he was diagnosed with Asperger's, only five years ago, has he dared say out loud that he is successful. Thanks to his persistence, through his strength of character, has he reached the position in life that he wants to be in. He is himself. That is what he also wants to teach other people with ASD: *'Be your true self and be honest.'*

AUTISME TEN TOP (AUTISM AT THE TOP)

The mission of *Autisme Ten Top* (Autism at the Top) is to improve the status in the job market of highly trained people with ASD, and to build a bridge between people with and without ASD.

Autisme Ten Top wants to achieve this by stimulating contact among fellow sufferers, and by improving the image of autism, social participation and job opportunities for people with autism. *Autisme Ten Top*, furthermore, wants to focus attention on moments of transition, such as the transition from secondary to higher vocational education or university, and then to work. Attention is also paid to changing jobs or change of activities within a job, as well as to the lifelong right to specialised career counselling.

OPPORTUNITIES ON THE WORKFLOOR FOR PEOPLE WITH ASD

- Autistic persons are honest and reliable. They have no hidden agenda.

- People with autism often have special skills and abilities that may be of interest to an employer, such as strong analytical skills, the ability to work long and with concentration on an assignment, cope efficiently with details, and having a considerable ability for innovation.

- People with autism often come up with original points of view and ideas on the way a goal can be achieved.

- People with autism are loyal; once their trust has been gained, an employer has an employee from whom he can benefit for years.

- People with autism often have a high level of self-awareness, with a creative, original, focused and intelligent outlook on life.

(Autisme Ten Top)

17.

SURVIVING IN A JUNGLE OF INFORMATION

Ben Kuijpers (46), self-proclaimed 'insight autistic', owner of the company 'I AM' and founder of the Annders Foundation, an organisation that helps people with an information processing disorder to use their qualities, enabling them to function independently in society by deploying their coping skills.

Ben Kuijpers has been diagnosed with seven different disorders, including fundamental depression, dyslexia and autism (both PDD-NOS and Asperger's). He has been a so-called 'problem case' since the age of six. At age 22, the doctors of the Dutch Industrial Insurance Administration Office told him that he would never again be able to rejoin the labour market. He didn't accept this and literally fought for his own life and the life of his two little girls. He did not win the fight for the latter. But the word 'bad luck' isn't part of his vocabulary. Ben finds strength and valuable experience in setbacks. This has made him the person he is today: A man who, thanks to his own experience, is able to help people make it through problems he has known at first hand himself. When other support workers run out of options, Ben is asked for advice.

Being 'at the end of one's tether' already says it all. There is a problem. But for whom? Is the person a problem for society, or is society a problem for the person? Or both? We will discuss it at length during this conversation. Ben was one such 'problem case' for a long time. In his book *Begrip Door Inzicht*[1] he describes his experiences and the important insights he has gained.

Ben was an unusual child. He asked questions that were not age-appropriate. He had the feeling that he could not be himself because people thought he was strange. He survived by playing roles that fitted into the group he was part of. It seemed as if he liked participating, but he was lonely. After primary school Ben attended junior technical school. He was popular with classmates, but was expelled from school for misbehaviour. A new school was found for him, and a period of relative peace and quiet followed. Ben finished school, went out a lot and met his girlfriend. But in his head there was no calm. He broke off his relationship and started self-mutilating. He writes in his book: 'The pains and fears became so intense that I lost it. I cut my left arm in several places and wrote "Help me" on the walls in blood.'

It was the start of a period of living in shelters and running away. He thought he could literally walk away from his problems, but the problems existed in his head and he always took them with him. Ben left for Canada, and came back. He was restless. Finally, he decided to block off all information coming from his feelings. A girl, Marie-Louise, managed to break through his mental armour. Ben fell in love and married her. Meanwhile, he had obtained his intermediate business education diploma in evening classes. He scraped his money together by going from one job to the next. The restlessness continued and he could not collect his thoughts. He writes: 'Many times the overview of my life had disappeared to such an extent that I couldn't make clear analyses any more. Arguments were running around in my head the whole day, but I almost couldn't close off any of them. I didn't have the situation under control any more. This scared me so much that I felt the need to end my life

---

1 'Kuipers, B. (2007) *Begrip Door Inzicht*. Antwerpen: Garant.

several times each day. For that was one of the few thoughts that I could hold.' Marie-Louise managed to convince Ben to seek professional help. For seven years he was counselled by a psychotherapist who advised him to follow a part-time higher professional training in personnel and employment. Ben completed this training. It rewarded him with more than just a diploma; it provided him with insight into his thought processes and the way he performs.

Despite his diplomas and newly acquired insights, Ben didn't succeed in finding a suitable job. Whenever he found one, he quickly got bored with his own tasks and started interfering with the work of others. His colleagues did not appreciate this, and considered him to be a nuisance. Ben was not accepted. *'I constantly had the feeling that they loathed me,'* he said during our conversation. The result was that he moved from one job to another. A positive aspect of this was that he really was himself during this period of his life. He stopped playing the roles that his social environment wanted him to play. He lifted his barricades to the outside world and looked for jobs in management consultancy, where his advice was actually appreciated. This took so much out of him, however, that he suffered severe burn-out. Ben became unable to move or talk. The physician treating him commented that his body's energy level was so low that the autonomous nervous system had switched off all superfluous functions: only the vital life functions were still active.

Ben picked himself up again. He wanted to move on in life. Marie-Louise became pregnant, and in 2001 their daughter Annette was born. The girl was born deaf, blind and with severe epilepsy. Due to a hereditary disease, her neurological system had not developed properly. Ben and his wife did all they could for their child, even though they knew that Annette would never grow old. They both stopped working, sold their house and used the equity to spend 100 per cent of their time with their daughter. Annette eventually reached the age of six-and-a-half, surviving for five years longer than the doctors had predicted. In 2005 Marie-Louise made a conscious choice to become pregnant again. Unfortunately, this child suffered from the same affliction. Ben and Marie-Louise decided to terminate the pregnancy after 18 weeks. They named the girl Vlinder (Butterfly).

Annette and Vlinder have had an important influence on Ben's development. He is complimented and respected by other people for the way he handled the difficult situation and the need to care for Annette. Several people told him afterwards that they had expected him to run away from the situation. But nothing was further from the truth. He analysed the events. This gave him some insight into the effect all this and what it meant to him. He felt that there was still some information missing and decided to have himself examined. After a few discussions with a psychiatrist, it was established that Ben had limitations falling within the autistic spectrum. At that point he knew that he couldn't change his mental problems. He could, however, work on reducing the consequences of his limitations. But it soon turned out not to be that simple. He started to delve into the subject of autism. He wanted to know what it said about him and reached a number of surprising, unorthodox conclusions, with the emphasis on 'unorthodox'.

Thanks to this investigation, he became not only a hands-on expert but also a specialist. In 2005 he was asked if he would be willing to use his experience and insights into his own limitations to help children with problems. He agreed right away. It fitted perfectly into his new life. During the first two years he worked via an agency. In March 2007 his own company 'I AM' opened its doors. He now counsels people with an information processing disorder. When other institutions are at their wits' end about how to help someone, Ben is asked for advice. It is important to him that these institutions come to him only at that stage. *'Because then the pedagogical norms do not apply any more,'* he says. *'I do it my way. I always take the person's point of view and take his or her perception seriously. People with a limitation are still too often approached with a view to their problems, with too little attention to their potential. The continuous emphasis on someone's mistakes leads to loss of confidence in itself and in the environment. It's no surprise that such a person will then start withdrawing from the world and resisting assistance. You don't even need to have a disability for that. It's better to help people find out what they can do and start working on their development from there. That eventually leads to more self-confidence and a decrease of negative behaviour.'*

Ben has reached the conclusion that the current diagnostic process is not good. *'A diagnosis doesn't actually say anything,'* he says. *'It is nothing more than an outcome of observed behaviour. You look at a consequence, but it says nothing about the cause. At first instance it may feel like a liberation, as it was for me. You think: at last I know. But because you don't want to be the exception, you start looking for ways to adapt to social norms. You quickly end up disillusioned. I also thought that I could adapt with the tips and the do's and don'ts provided to people with autism. That things would go better for me. Unfortunately, that was not the case.'*

Ben is convinced that he actually isn't autistic. *'I was diagnosed with having autism, but the reason why it might appear otherwise is the fact that I am highly gifted and highly sensitive.'* Ben has an IQ of 167 and an above-average level of empathy. He thinks there are many more people who are incorrectly diagnosed with autism. *'The psychologists and psychiatrists call the combination of autism and being highly gifted "Asperger's syndrome". But Hans Asperger never meant it like that. And the PDD-NOS diagnosis only means that the examiner doesn't know what's going on. PDD-NOS stands for: Pervasive Development Disorder Not Otherwise Specified. What does this mean? We see that someone clearly functions differently, but we cannot put our finger on it.'* According to Ben, these professionals had better focus on the question of where the specific characteristics they perceive come from, instead of trying to pigeon-hole them and establish a general treatment for it. *'If you score positively on eight out of the ten characteristics for a diagnosis, you have the jackpot, a diagnosis. But that doesn't say anything at all about the cause. If you don't know what the causes of the characteristics are, you shouldn't diagnose based on them. The fact is that you will then stigmatise on the basis of some negative assumptions. The diagnosis and the subsequent treatment plan consequently take the person's inabilities as a starting point, which is nonsense. Let's see what such a person can actually do. That is where the possibilities are to be found to help someone move forward. Map people's potential and help them out, starting from there.'* And it is of course important that we consider boundaries in this respect. You mustn't motivate people to continue in a direction where they become overstimulated.

According to Ben, changes in our society are responsible for an epidemic of autistics. He explains in detail what he means by this statement. *'Each child goes through an individual and a social development process. To begin with, during early primary school years, a child is self-centred. At the time the child moves on to secondary education they should be able to work with common learning goals. And they have to learn to take responsibility. That applied in the past and still applies now. In the past, the child was entirely surrounded by the safe and clear social boundaries provided by the school, the church, the family, the neighbourhood and social life. If you did not meet the social standards, you were corrected. A lot has changed in the past 15 to 20 years. The same social organisations are still active, but there is more tolerance and the child has been given more space. Children are corrected less promptly. Another development of the past 20 years is the arrival of 24-hour television, DVD-players, computers, games, internet and mobile phones. That flow of information is entirely lacking in any corrective instruments. What does it mean to a child when he is awarded 1000 points in a game for shooting someone's head off, while, in the school yard, he needs to behave properly? In some games, such as 'World of Warcraft,' you can acquire status. A 14-year-old child who has reached the highest level, enters a hallway where other warriors are lined up and bow to him. He may take a seat on a throne there. Half an hour later he is in the school yard where other children call out: "Hey, squinty, do you want me to conk you!" Many children have also lost insight into task and time. A child perceives ten minutes at the computer as totally different from ten minutes in class.'*

The old concept has totally disappeared and has been superseded and conquered by the new media. It is yet another proof of what the American scientist Marshall McLuhan claimed as long ago as in the 1960s: 'The medium is the message.' He assumed that modern means of communication such as radio, television and computers would come to have far-reaching sociological consequences, and that they would change the way we perceive the world. That is precisely what has happened, according to Ben. *'Children are at the end of their tether. What is good, what is bad, who are they, where are they compared to others, what can they expect? The old norms and values have disappeared, together with clarity and safety. That makes children anxious. They have to try and survive in a jungle of information. The behaviour of someone with autism is a direct consequence of this. That is what's wrong! Brain scans of young people show that their brains function in a totally different way than that of older generations. The same stimuli sometimes lead to activity in totally different areas of the brain. So the way information is processed in the brain has changed.'*

Ben has taken out his iPad to illustrate a few things. *'I am a visual thinker,'* he says. He shows part of a presentation he gave at a congress on autism in Antwerp. Ben likes to share his experiences and the insights he has acquired with others: parents, remedial teachers, support workers and psychologists. It is with that goal in mind that he founded the Annders Foundation. The name is composed from the names of his two daughters, Annette and Vlinder. The 's' is what links them to the target group on which the foundation focuses. Just like his children, this group is 'different'. They have a disorder in the way they process information. The name therefore also stands for 'perceiving differently'.

If, due to the current deluge of information, the risk increases of children (and adults) losing their way, what do we need to do? Is the education we currently offer our children even suitable any more? Secondary education pupils have a more than considerable dislike of school. It seems as if they don't understand what the education system demands of them. They find a lot of things they need to learn utterly pointless and useless. What does Ben think of that? *'The modern system of information provision is racing at 200 kilometres per hour on the highway, and the education system leisurely follows at 20 kilometres per hour. The new technological possibilities have changed society at warp speed, but the education system does not follow suit.'*

The number of dyslexics and people with ADHD is growing. A craze of a society with an overburdened information infrastructure. But according to Ben, these people are not abnormal at all. Meanwhile, the fact is that for the dyslexics, as well as the people with ADHD or with ASD, the curriculum needs to be adapted. In Ben's opinion it's impossible to keep this up. You can't demand this of instructors and teachers. Yet, especially in education, a lot can be done to make things clear once more for children. As far as Ben is concerned, this should start in the early years of primary education. *'First and foremost, it's important to give back to these children the homogeneity that was formerly the norm. Clear rules about what is and what isn't allowed. Clarity in what the children can actually expect. Reduce the chaos to insight. The children need to have this clarity before they reach the middle years of primary education. For at that point they have reached the age at which they start developing their own ego. By that stage children need to know what is expected of them and what it is like to take responsibility. If you have not laid the foundation there, you are too late.'* Ben doesn't mean that this clarity needs to be exacted from children by forbidding certain things. *'We need to take them seriously,'* he thinks. *'When, for example, after a fun day out they immediately dive into their computer games again, it is good to ask why they do that. You need to find out how they think. Don't judge the child, but try to find out what it experiences, as only then, can you reach and guide the child. Let's not be so arrogant as to think that we know it all.'* That is exactly where the problem lies, Ben thinks. The generation that determines what is good for the child actually doesn't have a clue what that child thinks. They come from a totally different era, a time when the information infrastructure was not yet overburdened. Education policy is also determined by that generation.

Back to autism, as that is what we came for, after all. By pigeon-holing people with autism, we stigmatise them. We are too focused on their limitations, trying to help them deal with those limitations, and pay too little attention to their talents and qualities. Ben has reached the conclusion that autism is an information processing disorder. *'That leads to a communication disorder, which in turn causes lack of insight. The lack of insight eventually leads to an integration disorder,'* Ben informs us. *'And lack of insight leads to fear, withdrawal or lapse – characteristics that we then call autism.'* Ben is not autistic, although he has actually been diagnosed as such. He is highly gifted, highly sensitive and a visual thinker. But aren't those pigeon-holes as well? What can these insights offer Ben himself? *'I see myself as a precursor of the current generation. My characteristics prevented me from understanding the world, and vice versa. I have tried to meet the norms of my environment. I didn't fully succeed and I was not accepted. Now, my characteristics are considered to be special and I am accepted. They practically give me the red-carpet treatment when I come,'* Ben laughs. *'I am lucky. If I wasn't highly gifted, I couldn't have made the analysis myself. I probably would not have made it then. I think that your life is not determined by what happens to you. It's determined by the choices you make the moment something happens to you. As a child, I was abused by a man for four years. My father died when I was 21. I have been loathed for years. I have had numerous different jobs. I have lost two children. My marriage broke down in July 2010 because my wife grieves for the loss of our children differently from me. We had been together for 21 years and I didn't know if I would make it on my own. All this together gives me reason enough to completely lose it. Nobody would have been surprised if I had derailed, if I had beaten up or even murdered people. Drug use, too – everybody would have understood that. But that didn't happen. I have chosen a different path and have refused to see myself as a victim. I have always looked for solutions and have continually taken responsibility for myself. I do not think that I have been unlucky in life. You can say all kinds of things about my life, but it isn't dull,'* he says with a smile.

Instead of becoming a psychiatric problem case, he chose the other option those six years ago: The role of analyst, advisor, hands-on expert and assistance worker. At first, he had to beg to be allowed to disseminate his views. Now, he is accepted and appreciated as an interpreter between persons with a disability and their environment. He is highly motivated. In the past two years he has worked 90-hour weeks to lay the foundation for his support work. Now, he is taking a step back. He is hired by support organisations, schools, the local educational advisory centre, and youth care agencies. He gives lectures, and coaches novice support workers. He helps people with problems by providing insight into the way things work for them, enabling them to move on. He has helped traumatised children, serious cases whom the regular care organisations couldn't help any more. By now, he has demonstrated for several children in special education that they can function at a normal level. *'These children actually do not belong in special education schools,'* Ben says. *'It doesn't make them better but worse, as they aren't challenged. They start playing up, taking dope, and become problem cases.'* According to Ben, children are placed in special schools too quickly. *'Children are too quickly deemed to have learning disabilities. Again, their qualities are not taken into account. The limitations are the focus of attention. Not enough effort is made to restore the self-confidence and self-respect of these children and dispel their anxieties. They need challenges and successful experiences. You need to approach them with respect and work with them on the basis of equality. That is what works.'* He doesn't understand why things are often done so differently in practice. For Ben, the focus is always on the person. Once, he even interrupted a conversation with the director of an institution when the child in question walked in. He knelt down to be at eye level with the child, and spoke to it. The director found this disrespectful, but Ben later explained to him what it was about. *'After all, I am here for the child and not for you. A child with problems only gives you one opportunity to come in. With you, I have several opportunities to present myself,'* he told the director. When you approach people from a position of authority, you will not get through to them, and will get hardly anything done.

18.

FROM DEVIL'S SPAWN TO PHILOSOPHER

Jan Verhaegh (67) has been married for 45 years to his wife Marietje and has a son and a daughter.

We pass a few people dressed as a clown, police officer and even as a banana when we enter Valkenburg (the Netherlands) where Jan Verhaegh lives. It is carnival season[1]. Jan and his wife Marietje also have a few festive paper chains hanging in the tree in their garden. For Jan himself it is not such a festive period. He has just had hip surgery and is walking on crutches. He is facing a few months of rehabilitation. But Jan is no less cheerful for that. During the conversation he makes grand remarks at which he laughs heartily. This, despite the many difficult times he has had during his life. His upbringing, in particular, has had a marked impact – even more, he says, than his autism ever had.

Jan is a former teacher, member of the board of the European Network of Users and Survivors of Psychiatry (www.enusp. org), as well as of Autism Europe (www.autismeurope.org). Jan is studying to obtain a MPhil in Psychiatry through an internet course provided by the University of Central Lancashire (UK). He has known for seven years that he has Asperger's.

---

1   Carnival is a Catholic feast by origin which also has pagan roots. It takes places in the three days preceding Ash Wednesday. People in the Netherlands often dress up and take to the streets during the celebrations.

Jan's father was farmer in south Netherlands. He raised a few cows and pigs and grew vegetables and fruit. He spent ten years living there with just his mother, Jan's grandmother, before he met Jan's mother. She then came to live on the farm. Jan is the eldest of the couple's children. Grandmother was increasingly left to look after the children while Jan's mother and father worked on the farm. The relationship between the three adults could be called strange. Jan's father had a very close bond with Jan's grandmother, which did not improve the relationship between the couple. They ended up in a kind of power struggle. For example, Jan's father did not kiss his wife when his mother was around. And while grandmother was spoiling the children, their mother wanted to raise them strictly. *'My grandmother would take me out of the playpen, and my mother would put me back in again,'* Jan says. *'My mother had to eat in the kitchen. My father ate with my grandmother in the living room. It was an endless conflict, very confusing. I often wondered why the animals on the farm were treated better than I was as a child. I was often scared, which made it difficult for me to concentrate in school.'*

One day, during a meeting of the Farmers' Wives Association, Jan's mother attended a lecture by a psychologist. It was about being overworked; she recognised herself in the portrait drawn, and addressed the psychologist during the break: 'You say that children of overworked mothers perform poorly at school. This could be the reason why Jan isn't doing well at school.' The psychologist advised her to take Jan to an educational advice centre in Venlo. He was put through all kinds of tests there. The conclusion? Jan might be very intelligent, but he was no good at school. Jan explains: *'If my mother had handled me more strictly, I would have behaved better, she was told. The problems I had were explained as a type of misbehaviour. I was disobedient and aggressive, a child of the devil. My mother was too soft on me. With my intelligence, I was a handful for my mother.'* Jan needed to learn to obey. But his parents weren't able to manage. And so, when Jan was eight-years-old, he was sent off to a Roman Catholic boarding school run by nuns. In the two years that followed, Jan learned how to obey and how to work. Crying was not allowed, and having feelings was absolutely forbidden. But the place did offer structure and safety. *'I thought: when I know these rules I am safe and they leave me alone. But I didn't understand some rules at all. The sister said, for example, that I had to lie with my hands on top of the blankets at night. I wondered about the reason for two days.'* The nuns were of the opinion they were doing disobedient, devilish children like Jan a favour. But according to Jan they were wrong. *'My autism was my first handicap. My upbringing was my second. Learning to suppress my feelings, in particular, was disastrous for my later emotional development.'*

Already as a child, Jan experienced being 'different' from other children. *'Why did I have to go to a convent and others didn't? I often felt guilty. I was a bad child. Other children were good. Why did I behave like that? But could I behave differently? No. I couldn't understand it at all. I often went to confession at the convent, but that didn't help either.'* Jan is emotional about the two years at the convent. We can see that he has almost gone back into that time. He thinks for a while and then says: *'Fortunately, they didn't abuse me sexually in the convent.'* Before we realise it, we end up discussing sexual abuse in the Roman Catholic church. Jan says: *'The sexual abuse in the church is a side effect. The real problem is that what the church considers to be good, is wrong. They consider absolute obedience a form of sanctity. With this obedience you conquer heaven. The Pope, for example, has accepted his suffering to the bitter end. Everything for God. The idea is that we must thank God for being able to participate in suffering, as this is what sets people free. The Church considers that a good thing, but precisely herein lies the evil. There is suppression. "Befehl ist Befehl (Command is Command)". If, within this balance of power, the flesh is stronger than the mind, this may lead to infantile forms of sexuality.'* So this type of Roman Catholicism had better be abolished? *'Yes!'* is Jan's immediate reply.

Jan came back to live at home again. Things were a little better but he continued to feel 'different'. He didn't have any friends, for example. Or did he? At age 15, he got to know a boy who had lost his mother. Jan understood what this boy was going through, as his own grandmother had died three years earlier. The boys sought each other's company. In several classes at school Jan also noticed that he was 'different' himself. Writing and drawing were no problem, but he was useless at all at subjects involving motor skills, such as handicraft, music and gymnastics. Jan points to a cupboard in his living room and says: *'Would you hand me those notebooks over there? My sister brought them with her this weekend. They are logbooks, look. Because I was so bad at gymnastics, I was excused from participating at some stage. When the others had gymnastics, I got a written assignment from the teacher. Just read it in these notebooks. That was a good idea.'*

At age 16, Jan had to take a number of aptitude tests. The conclusion was that he shouldn't choose a profession in which he would be dealing with people. *'What actually could I be? Lighthouse-keeper, archivist or forester in a forest where no poachers come.'* He laughs heartily and goes on: *'But my parents didn't take the tests too seriously. And I didn't know what to do with them either. Also, if you followed advanced elementary education, you went on to an office job, nursing or education. For me, it was teacher training college. I wanted to become a teacher.'* Although, at the time, Jan didn't yet know he had Asperger's, we wonder if it isn't difficult for someone with that disability to be a teacher. After all, a teacher is expected to communicate and interact with students and colleagues. Jan: *'It all worked out. I wasn't allowed to give gym classes. I was not bad at drawing and writing. At the teacher training college they didn't think I was abnormal. The students had a great time with me, just like you, Herman. As soon as you came in, you started laughing.'* We look at each other and feel, for the second time, that the conversation is taking a different turn. *'What is your training, Herman?'* Jan asks. *'Ah, biologist? That, too, is a social profession, isn't it? Tell me about yourself.'* Jan is all ears as Herman briefly talks about his own background. The tables have turned all of a sudden. *'Do you know,'* Jan continues, *'that it was discovered in psychiatry that the brain as such is social because its biological structure is plastic and can be affected both positively and negatively by social influences?'* A discussion develops about whether or not everything in biology is social. Nothing can live without something else, Jan and Herman conclude. Procreation, for example, is only possible through contact with others. It's impossible for things things to exist by themselves. Jan thinks, and says: *'Then Aristotle's narcissistic idea of God being supreme is impossible for biologists. What is the highest form of activity? Thinking. What does God do? God thinks about himself.'* Again a burst of laughter, in which we join in heartily. But enough about Aristotle – we return to Jan.

At age 18 Jan met his future wife, Marietje. They married three years later. Marietje quickly became pregnant, but then things went wrong. The child died immediately after birth. Marietje was in a bad way too. During labour, a nerve got trapped and she became paralysed on one side. Marietje was in hospital for a year. Jan says: *'In the Netherlands, children are still dying because the midwife won't go to the hospital in time. When we finally got to the hospital, our child was already dead. The paediatrician later said: "If a midwife hadn't attended the delivery, the child would have lived. It was a healthy child."'* Jan wasn't angry, nor did he cry when his child died. He had learned to control his feelings. A few days later he was back in the classroom. Everything seemed all right again. A year later, Marietje had physically recovered but fell into a depression. *'We then ended up with a psychologist, who helped us cope with the death of our child. Only after we had talked about it with him, did we dare think of having children again.'*

Jan enjoys studying and decided to get a secondary school teaching certificate, which qualifies him to teach at secondary schools. He could choose between history and theology. As he didn't want to learn numbers, he chose the latter. *'I fell off my chair with astonishment at the most irrational views people have. About the virgin birth of Jesus, for example. Theology is chock-full of fantasy.'* A few years later, Jan continued his studies at Nijmegen

University. He attended lectures on Marx's *Das Kapital* and the prophets of the Hebrew Bible. Marietje got pregnant again. Things went well and their second child was born. After three years of study, Jan decided to start working again. *'At university, they said that I could get a job there, but on one condition; I had to stop being active in the Dutch Communist Party (CPN). This party was in favour of revolution and wanted to put an end to oppression. That matched everything I knew about oppression and authority from my childhood; my parents, nuns, teachers and doctors.'* Jan didn't want to abandon his ideas. He left the university and found a job as a teacher at the school of domestic science and the school for secondary science education. *'I enjoyed that so much,'* he cries enthusiastically. *'Those girls were such fun.'* It was Jan's 'rebellious' period. He made his opinion clear in his lessons. He talked about freedom of speech and addressed the question of nuclear weapons policy. The authorities weren't too pleased with this. To avoid problems, Jan decided to apply at the Adult Education Centre in Valkenburg. He was offered a job.

As Marietje didn't want to move with their two children to Valkenburg (the Netherlands), Jan left for the south of the country by himself every Monday morning for two years, returning home again on Friday evenings. Jan was 36 by now and soldiered on, not having dealt with the traumas of his past and unaware that he had Asperger's. Two years later, he fell into a deep depression. *'Depression is autism's cup of sorrow. If you can't handle your autism, you become depressed,'* Jan explains. After six months he was admitted to day treatment in Venray for a year. *'By 1 August 1984, I had fully recovered again. We moved to Belgium and later to Valkenburg with the family. I also started work again.'* During this time Jan had psychotherapy. Things seemed to go all right but after seven years, in 1990, he had a relapse. Jan was once more admitted, now for a term of six months. Being off sick twice was not acceptable to the school governors. They wanted to get rid of Jan, but he didn't go quietly. *'The company medical officer advised me to call the union, which I did. They told me that I just had to go sit behind my desk and do nothing. I kept that up for nine months. It was quite cosy. My colleague in class often brought me coffee, while I dived into the works of Freud and Alice Miller behind my desk.'* Finally, the governors forbade Jan to come in any more. He ended up receiving benefit under the Disablement Insurance Act, started studying cultural sciences in Maastricht, and in 1997 became active in the patient movement.[2]

The years went by and then, in 2006, the penny dropped and people starting thinking of autism with reference to Jan. He says: *'My daughter studied psychology. One day she called me and said she suspected that I was autistic. The first thing I said was: "Has your boyfriend run away or something?" I thought it was a strange remark. She told me that she had had a lecture about autism. She recognised me in the story. We decided to go more deeply into the subject of autism. I also told my psychiatrist about my suspicion and he called in an autism expert. This man started to ask me questions such as: "Do you sometimes knock things over?" I then started laughing and said: "Yes, not ten minutes go by in which I don't knock something over." I was subsequently given two questionnaires to take home, one for myself and one for Marietje. I myself scored positive on sixty-five questions out of seventy. Marietje even had a score of seventy! So I asked my psychiatrist for assistance for my autism, but he didn't think that was a good idea. His treatment was good enough for me. During the time I was with him, I hadn't killed anyone, hanged myself or fallen back into a depression, after all. Furthermore, the causes of my problems lay in my childhood, according to my psychiatrist. Yes, that terrible youth, that was indeed true.'*

Then Marietje started to have problems. Her twin sister died, and she turned out to be allergic to household dust. Cleaning the house didn't work. Jan wanted to help but couldn't manage.

---

2   Patient movements – in the Netherlands – defend the interests of patients. This can be done by providing news, background information, experiences and contact. There are a lot of patient movements in the Netherlands for all kinds of diseases.

He contacted the GP and explained the problem. *'Thanks to my autism I appeared to be entitled to homecare. A home help was to teach me how to clean. She pinned notes all over the house with instructions about what I had to do, and in which order. There were more and more of them. After two years it drove me completely crazy. One day I smashed everything in the house out of pure frustration. The home help was terrified and yelled: "I'm shaking in my shoes next to a man weighing over 100 kilos. He may be doing worse things in a minute! What am I to do???" Eventually the psychiatrist was called in, which meant the end of me as housekeeper.'* Jan and Marietje started to receive help from other organisations, but had to pay thousands of euros out of their own pocket. Then they came in contact with the Dutch Regional Institution for Assisted Living. This organisation ensures that people with various psychiatric and psychosocial problems can live, function and participate in society as far as their condition allows, according to their own wishes and potential. *'But at some point, that ceased to work too. Marietje had a slight stroke. When she told the institution how much work she had looking after me, they said: "Then just get rid of Jan!" That was the last straw.'*

In July 2010 Jan and Marietje heard from the autism information centre in Heerlen that they were probably entitled to a so-called personal budget. *'But what do you think happened? No personal budget for me.'* Eventually, in January 2011, Jan finally managed to arrange it. Every week now, an autism expert coaches him for an hour and a half. Together they discuss what it means to have Asperger's and how to handle the problems.

So Jan has known since 2005 that he has Asperger's. What does that mean to him? *'It took from 1982 to 2005, so a full 23 years, for them to discover that I have a handicap. And when that had been proven, another five years passed before I received special autism assistance.'* That's sad, isn't it? *'It is. Many people of my age with autism are in permanent psychiatric treatment, considered untreatable. They take neuroleptics. I have been lucky in that regard.'* Could this have happened to him as well? He thinks for a while and says: *'I have Marietje. She has always supported me, and I her. She has a terrible history of incest. With me, she feels safe. I am not aggressive, as other lads can be sometimes.'* Jan has to think when we ask him if it is better to be diagnosed with Asperger's at a younger age. *'I wonder if sixteen-year-old children with Asperger's, for example, are admitted to teacher training college. A diagnosis may also have a stigmatising effect. People are excluded. Suppose I had known in my youth that I had Asperger's, I would probably not have gone to teacher training college and would't have become a teacher. How boring my life would have been then! I have now had many adventures, such as reading Freud behind a desk for nine months.'* So a diagnosis is stigmatising? *'No, that is not what I'm saying. If, in my youth, people had noticed what was actually wrong with me, I would have had coaching. I could have done without that severe depression. It's a good thing that children now get coaching. But there's still a question mark over whether or not this means they will be excluded from education paths and professions. There is provision of adapted jobs for deaf and blind people, but scarcely for people with autism.'*

Jan is on the board of the European Network of Users and Survivors of Psychiatry. Through this network he came into contact with the University of Central Lancaster in Preston, UK, which offers internet philosophy and psychiatry courses. The university wanted to make contact with clients to talk about various themes within these fields of study. Jan travelled to England and became interested in philosophy. He decided to resume studying, via the internet this time. *'I still need to finish a paper of 8,000 words, for which I get help from Professor Jim van Os among others. This professor has been elected for the fourth time by his colleagues as the top psychiatrist in the Netherlands. He also pays for my studies. When the paper is finished, I can call myself Master of Philosophy or Psychiatry,'* Jan tells us with some pride. We ask Jan why exactly he chose to study philosophy. *'As a child, I always read lots of books. Philosophy is abstract. I can think about the world in an abstract way. A novel is more complicated. Furthermore, people with Asperger's face the impossible task of getting their head to respond to things they cannot sense. You can't think about things you can't feel. Impossible. Yet they still have to try. So as a child, I was already thinking a lot about, for example, why animals are treated better than human beings.'*

From devil's spawn to philosopher; we call Jan successful. But does he think he is as well? He sighs: *'You know, suppose you are blind, have no help and are moving through city traffic. If, by the end of the day, you are still alive, would you call yourself successful or simply lucky? Autism is and continues to be a serious handicap. You don't understand yourself. I am 67 now, and have survived. I am on the board of the European Network of Users and Survivors of Psychiatry and of Autism Europe. I have done great things from which people with Asperger's will probably be excluded in the future. Does that make me successful?'* We ask Jan if he is happy. *'I have been pretty unhappy for the greater part of my life. I have suffered a lot from depressions. I have continually tried to do the impossible, such as understanding things I cannot understand. Think of functioning in society. In addition, I wonder if I haven't suffered more from my upbringing than from my autism. Due to that upbringing, I couldn't come to terms with anything, such as the death of my child. Doctors tried to turn a child of the devil into a little angel. What they considered to be good, has to be described as evil. Such a dark upbringing is very harmful to people. Hegel says: "Wir sollen den Eigenwillen des Kindes brechen (We must break down the child's self-will)." Terrible.'* We want to draw the conversation to an end, but Jan muses on: *'Kant, now, he was fun! At age 70 he was still able to weep about his upbringing. He understood things. Kant respected children. And Marx! He had a lot of love for them. He had eight himself.'* We watch as Jan thinks and finally says: *'Society should be more autism- and child-friendly.'*

Jan Verhaegh – his life has not always been easy, and still is not always. But with his perseverance and generous sense of humour he has still achieved a lot. He is a beautiful person, this philosopher.

19.

'EINSTEIN HAD ASPERGER'S, DIDN'T HE?'

Mark Ty-Wharton (50), also known as Mark Tinley, has Asperger's and is a British writer and musician.

We took the train to Biggleswade, about one hour from Kings Cross Station in London, where Mark Ty-Wharton is waiting for us. From the small train station it's only a five-minute walk to his house. In his kitchen, we sit in medieval-like chairs, drink tea and listen to his story. Mark is known for his work in music and writing. He has played guitar in several bands (and still does), and produced music by Duran Duran, Adamski, Gary Numan and others. After being diagnosed with Asperger's syndrome in 2006 he gave up his career in the music industry, and now he follows his passion for writing. His books so far have been read by more than 50,000 people.

When we talk about his Asperger's Mark, tells us that he is capable of reducing his level of disability, which some specialists think is not possible for people with Asperger's syndrome to do. *'I'm convinced that I'm capable of learning to read facial expressions, for instance,'* Mark says. *'First I have to accept that I am not good at it, and then I can do something about it. It's difficult but it's mainly learning a new habit. There are also people with Asperger's who learn to imitate expression in voices by listening to talk shows. One person even copied the voice of the talk show host Howard Stern. Now he sounds just like him, which is a bit weird, of course. My voice also sounded flat but I have learned to improve my speaking by modulating my voice, with the help of voice coaches. It improved my self-confidence, now I speak for groups of people. I've learned to look people in the eye when I am talking to them. In 1999 I followed a course with a company called Landmark Education. I also did the advanced course. I remember that there were 120 people in a room, lined up in front of each other. We had to stare into each other's eyes. If you do that all day, you ask yourself: what is the problem with looking people in the eye? There is no problem any more. Before that I drove people nuts because I didn't look them in the eye when they spoke to me or when I spoke to them.'*

Mark has always been different. Now he is old and experienced enough not to let it bother him. On the contrary, he might even make it a trademark in some way. But when he was much younger it made him self-conscious. *'I'd be deliberately different, to hide the fact that I was different. I didn't want people to find out that I was sort of odd. So I was chaotic and musical and creative. I did strange things so people thought: wow, he is different. I played a character. I was more drunk than anyone else, I played the guitar louder than anyone else. It worked for me. The strange thing is that since I've been diagnosed with Asperger's, some friends come to me and say: "You can't possibly have Asperger's." But I'm not going to argue about it.'*

There were no problems until Mark was seven-years-old. He was a quick learner. He learned the alphabet so quickly that he was let out to play a long time before the other children. So he ended up playing mostly on his own. When he was seven his parents sent him to another school. There, he was so much ahead of the other pupils that he skipped two classes. After one year with children who were two years his senior, he stayed in the same class, making the age difference with the other pupils just one year. Then the school merged with another school, and everything changed again. They put him in a class with pupils of his own age. The switches were difficult for Mark. He got bored doing the same lessons again and again and started messing around. Mark: *'But I didn't have significant social problems. I moulded myself into this character that was going to be a pop star. And everybody in the school believed it. When I was eight or nine I used to steal nail varnish from the chemist and went to school with my nails painted silver. And I sprayed my shoes silver. I wore makeup too. My parents' friends were irritated by it. But it felt cool. I was also being disruptive at school and wasn't afraid of the teacher. That kept me safe from the bullies. I wasn't in any particular group, and managed to stay in with all of them. And the girls liked me because I was playing in a band.'*

Mark seems to have had a happy youth. He was less lucky when he got older. From the age of 13 he started suffering from panic attacks and anxiety. *'Social anxiety,'* Mark explains. *'For instance, when I entered a place I didn't know with strangers. But I didn't realise what was happening to me. I suffered from chronic bronchitis when I was a small child as well, and poor breathing habits might have been the cause of the panic attacks.'* The panic attacks got worse as Mark grew older. When he went to see the doctor he was sent home with a relaxation tape and a ten-step anxiety programme. The result was that he learned to relax, but it didn't help him when he was back amongst people. At that point he got the feeling that something was wrong with him. Mark: *'The doctor didn't explain what anxiety was, and I didn't understand where it came from.'* He also spent thousands of pounds seeing alternative therapists, and even hypnotists. He found himself lying in a chair with a hypnotist telling him that he was an egg, and then she hit him hard on the forehead to crack him open to find out what was wrong with him. All it did was cost him a lot of money.

One of Mark friends started having panic attacks. He was worried about her. After a couple of years he asked his friend how she was doing with her panic attacks. *'She told me she was feeling better. I couldn't understand that. I believed that panic attacks must go on for ever.'* Other friends, too, stopped having panic attacks. Mark continues: *'One of them was a model. She had a lot of problems modelling for over a year, started having panic attacks. I was really surprised when they stopped.'* In 2006 Mark decided to be assessed. Why had they stopped having those attacks and he didn't? He wanted to know! First he was examined for ADD, but that turned out not to be his problem. After seeing Stephen Fry talking about his bipolar disorder on television, he rang his doctor to say that he wanted an assessment for bipolar disorder. But the assessment came to nothing. *'The psychologist wrote me a letter after he had seen me. There a lot of mistakes in it. So I wrote him a six-page – very pedantic and literal – letter, saying amongst others that my name is Mark TinLey, not Mark TinNey! I corrected all his spelling.'* When Mark saw the next psychologist, this one looked at the letter and said: 'Only somebody with Asperger's would do something like that!' So that was part of the diagnosis. Then Mark's partner read about Asperger's on the internet. Mark remembered seeing some guy on television talking about his Asperger's, who said: 'I have no feelings for my wife and children,' and thought: that's not me. Mark has strong feelings for his partner and his children. In the end, a psychiatrist tested Mark on several disorders and found out that Mark is unable to read facial expressions. He 'discovered' that Mark met several of the criteria for a diagnosis of Asperger's. Mark wasn't too sure at first, but after reading a few books and visiting social groups for adults with Asperger's, he recognised some of his traits in others and became more convinced. Mark: *'When I went to social groups I expected to meet all kinds of weird people, but most people seemed to socialise quite normally. Just like me. People with Asperger's create reference points for social situations, like sitting at my kitchen table and talking to you. I have done this before, so I know what to expect and everything will be fine. But for some situations we don't have reference points. If you two had been talking between yourselves and knew something that I don't, it would be very confusing for me, as at that point I am not able to process what is happening and I may start to get worried. I think it's all practice and experience. When I was younger I felt uncomfortable in crowds or standing in queues in the supermarket. I avoided those situations, I stayed at home as much as possible. Until a friend taught me to see all those people as grains of sand, like being on a beach. Another thing I didn't like was being on the London Underground. I always had a book with me and tried to concentrate my attention on what I was reading, to distract me from the fact that I was on a train. It was a real effort.'*

Mark now thinks that his anxiety is caused by too much sensory stimulation. Mark: *'When I have a busy week and I go to bed on Friday, it's like I'm lying under the floodlights in a full football stadium. But the light is inside my head. It's diagnosed as anxiety, but may be it's not anxiety. It's Asperger's. It happens if I have too much strenuous social interaction, like this interview. I mustn't do this every day. On the other hand, I am very driven. Sometimes I have to go to social events like club nights because I can meet interesting people to work for, or work with. I never relish the idea of going there. I have to push myself, and most of the time, if it's important, I go.'*

There was a period in Mark's life when he was drinking too much. It was a sort of remedy for anxiety. When he drank he had less trouble leaving his house and socialising. At some point he realised that he was on the wrong track, and stopped drinking. Instead, he used all kinds of Chinese herbs for his anxiety. He was offered two jobs simultaneously. One was to produce a record for Everything But The Girl in a studio. The other was to go on world tour with the band Duran Duran. He deliberately chose the more difficult one: the world tour. Mark: *'I went to the Middle East and I thought: I can't go back now. So I focused on my work and did the best I could. I tried to find time and places where I could be quiet. People were always asking my why I looked worried. The thing that echoes through my head all my life is people asking: "Are you all right? You look really upset." It wasn't that, I was angry, I was just sitting quietly somewhere. But it was the usual reaction when people saw me. When I came back to London after eight months I was sitting on the train and realised: this is strange, I'm on the train and I don't feel any panic. I was so happy that I started singing.'*

Although he doesn't, Mark could call himself successful in music and writing. *'I have worked on five albums by Duran Duran, and one of the records sold two million copies. I was paid for that. But when I think about it I realise that there's always a drive to do something else. It feels like I'm always a bit in someone else's shadow. And it feels as if I should be able to be really socially outgoing, but that social aspect is what is missing. That makes the difference between where I am and a really big star. But I am learning. Twenty years ago, I couldn't leave my house to meet people at the train station or buy milk at the supermarket. My success story is that, within a certain amount of time, I've become able to live a social life to a certain degree. If I didn't have anxiety I might have achieved more. To be socially inept is not necessarily a problem. If you're socially inept but still can be with people, it doesn't bother you. So you can still be successful. Einstein had Asperger's, didn't he? There are all kinds of people. Asperger's is just one facet of diversity.'*

EPILOGUE

December 2013. The book is finished. But we realise that this book will never be complete. There are many more other stories to be written. Like the story of Diederik Weve (53), which ran in the Dutch paper *NRC Handelsblad* on 15 June 2011. Diederik is an engineer and works at Shell. He has Asperger's, but has only known it for two years. *'If I had been diagnosed sooner, they might have stopped pushing me to follow the standard career path,'* he says. He went to look for colleagues with autism but didn't find any, although there are about a thousand worldwide working at Shell. He thinks they are afraid to tell, due to the existing stereotype of autistics as all being mentally disabled. The taboo linked to autism stimulates inefficiency, the engineer thinks, as autistics are assessed only on their weak points, and not on their qualities. His 'Autistics out of the Closet' campaign at Shell has by now yielded four fellow autistics. 'Onward to ten,' he optimistically tells the paper.

Diederik's story sounds familiar. It fits in with this book. And there are many more stories like that. This book is the tip of an iceberg, but one that is slowly but surely melting. Diederik Weve starts a campaign to break the taboo on autism at Shell. He is a pioneer, but fortunately not the only one. Everyone with autism who allowed us to tell their story in this book, is a pioneer. And we want to express our heartfelt thanks to them.

We would like briefly to single out two of them. As we write these last words, Carlo Post and Jaap Brand are busy organising an extensive image campaign for employers. They aim to break the stereotypic image of autism, and to ensure that people with autism are offered more opportunities on the job market.

And if you really want to know what AutiPower! is, we would like to draw your attention to the following. In June

2010 the Intelligent Community Forum (ICF), an international think tank in the field of economic and social development, proclaimed the Eindhoven region (in the Netherlands) the cleverest in the world. In that same month, a study by the British autism specialist Simon Baron-Cohen was presented in the news. It turned out that autism is twice as common in the Eindhoven region as in the rest of the Netherlands.

Say no more!

Herman Jansen and Betty Rombout